# Review of International Regulatory Co-operation of the United Kingdom

This document, as well as any data and map included herein, are without prejudice to the status of or sovereignty over any territory, to the delimitation of international frontiers and boundaries and to the name of any territory, city or area.

The statistical data for Israel are supplied by and under the responsibility of the relevant Israeli authorities. The use of such data by the OECD is without prejudice to the status of the Golan Heights, East Jerusalem and Israeli settlements in the West Bank under the terms of international law.

**Please cite this publication as:**
OECD (2020), *Review of International Regulatory Co-operation of the United Kingdom*, OECD Publishing, Paris, *https://doi.org/10.1787/09be52f0-en*.

ISBN 978-92-64-71554-7 (print)
ISBN 978-92-64-56660-6 (pdf)
ISBN 978-92-64-62835-9 (HTML)
ISBN 978-92-64-88831-9 (epub)

**Photo credits:** Cover © Artistdesign29/Shutterstock.com.

Corrigenda to publications may be found on line at: *www.oecd.org/about/publishing/corrigenda.htm*.
© OECD 2020

The use of this work, whether digital or print, is governed by the Terms and Conditions to be found at *http://www.oecd.org/termsandconditions*.

# Foreword

New opportunities and changes brought by globalisation present contemporary policy makers and regulators with challenges that cannot be dealt with in isolation. Against this backdrop, international regulatory co-operation (IRC) provides an opportunity for countries, and in particular domestic regulators, to consider the impacts of their regulations beyond their borders, expand the evidence for decision making, learn from the experience of their peers and develop concerted approaches to challenges that transcend borders. IRC can be particularly useful for the United Kingdom in this pivotal time for its regulatory policy agenda. Like other countries across the globe, the United Kingdom is facing the daunting challenge of regulating in a fast-paced, digital and interconnected world. At the same time, with the United Kingdom's recent withdrawal from the European Union, departments and regulators are likely to take on additional responsibilities that formerly belonged to European institutions, and the UK government to rethink its engagement with international peers.

This report documents the context of IRC policies and practices in the United Kingdom, unilateral efforts for embedding international considerations in domestic regulatory process as well as the bilateral, regional or multilateral co-operative efforts on regulatory matters. In addition it provides a sample of IRC in practice with four case studies on financial services, nuclear energy, medical and healthcare products, and product safety. At a time when IRC is increasingly essential for countries to address transboundary policy challenges and remains a largely untapped tool, the recommendations made to the United Kingdom in this review can offer valuable lessons to other countries within the OECD and beyond.

This report is the second in-depth international regulatory co-operation review undertaken by the OECD, following the review of IRC in Mexico conducted in 2018. By requesting such a review, the UK pushes forward the boundaries of regulatory policy and showcases the new international dimension of regulation that can no longer be ignored. The OECD 2012 *Recommendation of the Council on Regulatory Policy and Governance* makes IRC an integral part of quality regulation in today's globalised context. And yet, the OECD's extensive analytical work, horizontal surveys and specific country and sector studies on IRC developed since 2012 confirm IRC is still largely an untapped tool across OECD countries. By highlighting the benefits of IRC for the United Kingdom today, this review confirms the IRC as a key pillar for regulatory policy and governance in the 21$^{st}$ century.

The review was carried out by the OECD Public Governance Directorate under the auspices of the OECD Regulatory Policy Committee using the regulatory policy review methodology developed over two decades of peer learning. It is based on information gathered namely through interviews with authorities from the Government of United Kingdom, private sector and academia in London in December 2018, March and September 2019. Two preliminary versions of the report were discussed in policy workshops with a wide range of United Kingdom public and private sector representatives. This report was peer reviewed by the OECD Regulatory Policy Committee, approved on 7 November 2019 and prepared for publication by the OECD Secretariat.

# Acknowledgements

This study was prepared by the OECD Public Governance Directorate (GOV) under the leadership of Marcos Bonturi, Director, and Nick Malyshev, Head of the Regulatory Policy Division in GOV. It was co-ordinated and drafted by Céline Kauffmann and Marianna Karttunen, with substantial inputs from Richard Alcorn and Guillermo Hernández, from the OECD Regulatory Policy Division. The authors are grateful for guidance from the Director's Office of the Public Governance Directorate, including Janos Bertok, Acting Director, Klas Klaas and Andrea Uhrhammer. The report was prepared for publication by Jennifer Stein and administrative assistance was provided by Claudia Paupe.

The assessment by peers with unique experience on IRC was instrumental in designing the key conclusions and recommendations of this report. The OECD Secretariat is very grateful for the invaluable inputs provided by Jeannine Ritchot, former Executive Director of the Regulatory Policy and Cooperation Directorate from the Treasury Board (Canada); Julie Nind, Principal Policy advisor at the Ministry of Business, Innovation and Employment (New Zealand); and Dag Arne Aarnes, Director of Better Regulation Council (Norway).

Special thanks go to the United Kingdom Department for Business, Energy and Industrial Strategy (BEIS) and its staff, in particular to Jaee Samant, Carl Cresswell, Chris Carr, Ruth Harriford, Kim Wager, Nick Morgan, Emily Wykes, and Jonathan Evans for their support and insights throughout the review process.

We also express our sincere gratitude to the many government and non-government officials who provided inputs during the year-long development process, who participated actively in the three workshops that structured the work and who shared their views on the successive drafts of the report. They include representatives from the Better Regulations Executive, the British Standards Institute, the Department for Digital, Culture, Media and Sports, the Department for International Trade, the Departmental Better Regulation Units, Department for Environment, Food and Rural Affairs, the UK Environment Agency, the Financial Conduct Authority, the Food Standards Authority, the Foreign and Commonwealth Office, the Health and Safety Executive, Her Majesty's Treasury, Intellectual Property Office, Medicine and Healthcare products Regulatory Authority, National Audit Office, Office for Product Safety and Standards, Office of Communications, Office of Gas and Electricity Markets, Office for Nuclear Regulation, UK Regulatory Policy Committee and United Kingdom Accreditation Service. The report also benefitted from insights from representatives from the British Chamber of Commerce, the Confederation of British Industry, Federation of Small Businesses, the Institute of Directors, Make UK, NESTA and academics from the London School of Economics.

# Table of contents

Abbreviations and acronyms 8

Executive summary 11

Key terms used in the report 13

1 Context of IRC policies and practices 15
    Regulatory production in the United Kingdom and broad regulatory policy context 16
    Institutional context 18
    Existing policy and guidance embedding considerations of IRC 23
    References 25
    Notes 26

2 Embedding the international environment in the rule-making machinery 27
    Scope of better regulation in the United Kingdom: domestic focus, with European considerations 28
    International considerations within regulatory impact assessments (RIA) 32
    Consideration of international instruments 33
    Stakeholder engagement 34
    Post-implementation reviews 37
    Regulatory delivery 39
    References 42
    Notes 44

3 Regulatory co-operation practices and tools 47
    The traditional UK international co-operation instruments: treaties and Memoranda of Understanding 48
    Exchange of information and technical assistance 49
    The building of new co-operation capacities: trade and mutual recognition agreements 50
    UK participation in regional *fora* 52
    UK participation in multilateral *fora* 54
    References 55
    Notes 56

## 4 Sectoral case studies — 58
　Financial services — 59
　Nuclear energy — 63
　Medical and healthcare products — 68
　Product safety — 71
　References — 75
　Notes — 76

## 5 Assessment and recommendations — 79
　General overview of international regulatory co-operation (IRC) in the United Kingdom — 80
　Key priority areas of focus for the United Kingdom on IRC — 81
　Reference — 97
　Notes — 98

## Annex A. What is international regulatory co-operation (IRC)? — 99

## Annex B. Sectoral coverage of mutual recognition agreements of EU — 103

### Tables

Table 4.1. UK Fintech bridge agreements — 61
Table 4.2. UK authorities represented in selected international organisations dealing with financial regulation — 63
Table 4.3. UK bilateral regulatory co-operation in the nuclear energy sector — 66
Table 4.4. MHRA's bilateral regulatory co-operation agreements — 70

### Figures

Figure 1.1. United Kingdom Performance on core regulatory management tools — 17
Figure 1.2. Institutions involved in overseeing and conducting IRC — 19
Figure 2.1. Regulatory measures under the scope of UK Better Regulation — 30
Figure 2.2. Better regulation phases in the United Kingdom — 31
Figure 2.3. International references in BSI standards — 34
Figure 3.1. United Kingdom: exports to and imports from main partner countries — 50
Figure 3.2. Total UK trade — 50

Figure A A.1. The variety of IRC approaches — 100

### Boxes

Box 1.1. UK Rulemaking: definitions of regulatory instruments and standards — 16
Box 1.2. Better Regulation Units — 20
Box 1.3. Regulatory diplomacy — 21
Box 1.4. Composition of the Reducing Regulation Sub-Committee (RRC) — 22
Box 1.5. UK White Paper on "Regulation for the Fourth Industrial Revolution" — 24
Box 2.1. Types of regulatory bodies in the United Kingdom — 29
Box 2.2. United Kingdom Consultation Principles 2018 — 35
Box 2.3. Notification of technical regulations to the European Commission by EU member States — 36
Box 2.4. Post Implementation Review Template — 38
Box 3.1. Participation in EU bodies: the example of telecoms — 53
Box 4.1. ONR's Framework for International Engagement — 64
Box 4.2. Selected examples of UK multilateral regulatory co-operation in the nuclear energy sector — 67
Box 5.1. Whole of government strategy and organisation of IRC: experiences from Canada and New Zealand — 84
Box 5.2. The IRC drivers — 85

Box 5.3. Norway adoption and implementation of EU legislation                                                                85
Box 5.4. Embedding IRC in regulatory management tools: the example of Canada and New Zealand                                 88
Box 5.5. How is the need to consider international standards and other relevant regulatory frameworks
conveyed in other jurisdictions                                                                                              89
Box 5.6. Regulatory Co-operation in Canada: a credit under one-in, one-out                                                   90
Box 5.7. Embedding IRC in ex post reviews in Canada and in Trans-Tasman co-operation                                         90
Box 5.8. Forward planning as a tool to inform domestic and foreign stakeholders in other jurisdictions                       92
Box 5.9. Structuring communities of regulatory practices in Canada and New Zealand                                           94
Box 5.10. Examples of international Regulatory Cooperation Fora related to trade agreements                                  96
Box 5.11. Collecting views from stakeholders for more targeted IRC                                                           97

Box A A.1. IRC in practice: examples of approaches and related benefits                                                     101

# Abbreviations and acronyms

| | |
|---|---|
| AAR | Accelerated access review |
| ANZLF | New Zealand and Australia Leadership Forum |
| ANZSOG | Australia and New Zealand School of Government |
| BEIS | Department for Business, Energy and Industrial Strategy |
| BEREC | Body of European Regulators for Electronic Communication |
| BoE | Bank of England |
| BRE | Better Regulation Executive |
| BRUs | Better Regulation Units |
| BSI | British Standards Institution |
| CABs | Conformity assessment bodies |
| CAPs | conformity assessment procedures |
| CDR | Cabinet Directive on Regulation |
| CETA | Comprehensive Economic and Trade Agreement |
| CFDA | China Food and Drug Administration |
| CFR | Community of Federal Regulators |
| CFTC | Commodity Futures Trading Commission |
| CPTPP | Comprehensive and Progressive Agreement for Trans-Pacific Partnership |
| CSS | Commission on Safety Standards |
| CUSMA | Canada-United States-Mexico Agreement |
| Defra | Department for Environment, Food, and Rural Affairs |
| DIT | Department for International Trade |
| EA | European Accreditation Cooperation |
| EC | European Commission |
| EEA | European Economic Area |
| EFTA | European Free Trade Association |
| EMA | European Medicines Agency |
| ESARDA | European Safeguards Research and Development Association |
| ESMA | European Securities and Markets Authority |
| FATF | Financial Action Task Force |
| FCA | Financial Conduct Authority |

| | |
|---|---|
| FCO | Foreign and Commonwealth Office |
| GFIN | Global Financial Innovation Network |
| GFPs | Global Financial Partnerships |
| GMP | Good Manufacturing Practice |
| G-REG | Government Regulatory Practice Initiative |
| GRP | Good Regulatory Practices |
| HSE | Health and Safety Executive |
| IAEA | International Atomic Energy Agency |
| IAF | International Accreditation Forum |
| ICMRA | International Coalition of Medicines Regulatory Authorities |
| IEAs | Information Exchange Arrangements |
| IEC | International Electrotechnical Commission |
| ILAC | International Laboratory Accreditation Cooperation |
| IMF | International Monetary Fund |
| IOs | International organisations |
| IOSCO | International Organization of Securities Commissions |
| IPPAS | International Physical Protection Advisory Service |
| IRC | International regulatory co-operation |
| IRRS | International Atomic Energy Agency's Integrated Regulatory Review Service |
| ISO | International Organization for Standardization |
| MDEP | Multinational Design Evaluation Programme |
| MHRA | Medicines and Healthcare Products Regulatory Agency |
| MMoU | Multilateral Memorandum of Understanding |
| MoUs | Memoranda of Understanding |
| MRAs | Mutual Recognition Agreements |
| NANDO | New Approach Notified and Designated Organisations |
| NAO | National Audit Office |
| NCAs | Nuclear Cooperation Agreements |
| NDPBs | Non-Departmental Public Bodies |
| NEA | Nuclear Energy Agency |
| NIA | Nuclear Industry Association |
| NII | National Information Infrastructure |
| NMDs | Non-Ministerial Departments |
| NSGC | Nuclear Security Guidance Committee |
| ONR | Office for Nuclear Regulation |
| OPSS | Office for Product Safety and Standards |
| OSCE | Organization for Security Co-operation in Europe |
| PC | Productivity Commission |
| PIR | Post-Implementation Review |

| | |
|---|---|
| **PRA** | Prudential Regulation Authority |
| **PSR** | Payment Systems Regulator |
| **RCC** | Regulatory Cooperation Council |
| **RCF** | Regulatory Cooperation Forum |
| **RIA** | Regulatory impact assessment |
| **ROAMEF** | Rationale, Objectives, Appraisal, Monitoring, Evaluation and Feedback |
| **RPC** | Regulatory Policy Committee |
| **RRC** | Reducing Regulation Sub-Committee |
| **SAGSI** | Standing Advisory Group on Safeguards Implementation |
| **SBEE** | Small Business, Enterprise and Employment |
| **SFC** | Securities and Futures Commission |
| **SMR** | Small Modular Reactor |
| **SPS** | sanitary and phytosanitary |
| **TBS** | Treasury Board Secretariat of Canada |
| **TBT** | technical barriers to trade |
| **TTMRA** | Trans-Tasman Mutual Recognition Arrangement |
| **UKAS** | United Kingdom Accreditation Service |
| **UKAS** | United Kingdom Accreditation Service |
| **WTO** | World Trade Organization |

# Executive summary

The overwhelming pace of technological change and the unprecedented interconnectedness of economies present governments with uncertainty and complexity in terms of what and how to regulate. In such a context, international regulatory co-operation (IRC) has become a critical dimension of regulatory quality and effectiveness. This reality, as well as the withdrawal of the United Kingdom from the European Union (EU), have a significant effect on the United Kingdom's rulemaking landscape. Developing a strong IRC strategy has become particularly critical to help the United Kingdom ensure that rulemaking remains adapted to the global context in which the country operates.

This *Review on International Regulatory Co-operation* analyses and builds on the strong regulatory policy framework established by the United Kingdom to identify where and how international considerations and co-operation can be further embedded in rulemaking to avoid undue inconsistencies and support regulatory effectiveness. This review takes a medium- to longer-term view of the reforms that the United Kingdom could bring to its rulemaking systems to encompass greater international considerations and does not focus strictly on the short-term discussions on the EU withdrawal. These pivotal times for the United Kingdom come with a strong opportunity to revisit traditional better regulation disciplines, including more systematically considering the broader regulatory environment beyond the EU and the single market. With the United Kingdom already playing a leading role in regulatory policy and international co-operation, it is only natural for it to engage more actively in IRC.

The study starts by setting the scene with an overview of the context of IRC policies and practices (Chapter 1). It then reviews the rulemaking machinery to identify the entry points for IRC (Chapter 2). Chapter 3 presents the co-operation practices and tools used by departments and regulators. In Chapter 4, four specific sector case studies (financial services, nuclear energy, medical and health products, and product safety) illustrate various IRC practices and challenges. Finally, building on the in-depth understanding of the UK rulemaking activities provided by previous chapters, the report offers recommendations to strengthen IRC.

The United Kingdom has been a leader in regulatory policy among OECD countries for years. It has well-established regulatory disciplines, cross-government policies providing incentives for a range of regulators to pursue common objectives and various actors supporting and overseeing the conduct of regulatory policy. However, IRC is still implicitly rather than overtly embedded in the United Kingdom's existing institutional and policy framework for regulatory policy. A multiplicity of actors are involved in the conduct of IRC, but none is clearly tasked with its oversight, and there is no common narrative or policy to catalyse these various actors' energy. This results in an *ad hoc* approach to IRC, both in the unilateral regulatory process and the UK's bilateral, regional and multilateral co-operative efforts.

There are various "entry points" for IRC in the United Kingdom's regulatory process, offering regulators "unilateral" opportunities to embed international considerations in their rulemaking. In particular, the country's former membership in the European Union entailed a strong anchoring in EU legislation, the embedding of international standards in UK British standards (in particular via European standards) and mechanisms to prevent undue trade impacts of UK regulations for other EU countries (e.g. through the notifications of draft regulations to the EU Commission and a common conformity assessment and accreditation system). In addition, the United Kingdom better regulation agenda also has several entry points for taking into account the international context more broadly. International instruments and overseas practices are sometimes considered in the context of identifying various alternatives to address a specific policy challenge. A new RIA template, with an international trade and investment-related question, is also under trial. Post-implementation reviews may be used to identify how a domestic measure's impact compares to different approaches followed abroad.

Historically, the United Kingdom has actively co-operated internationally on laws and regulations as well as on regulatory policy. It does so through bilateral engagement with foreign peers through traditional co-operation tools (Treaties, Memoranda of Understanding) and through participation in numerous international organisations and initiatives, at many levels of government. A large portion of the country's international co-operation efforts, such as those related to trade, were under the auspices of the EU, leaving UK bodies with less initiative in this respect. Beyond this, and even when the rulemaking competence did remain largely at the member state level, UK regulators were integrated in a number of EU initiatives, networks and agencies.

The United Kingdom's withdrawal from the EU places a new responsibility on the United Kingdom for repatriating a number of regulatory functions, establishing the cooperation needed to fill the potential losses of privileges and designing a trade policy to address the trade costs of regulatory divergences with both EU members and other trading partners. The EU remains the UK's first partner in many regulatory areas, and thus close co-operation will likely continue between the EU and the UK. However, the withdrawal from the EU will likely influence the terms of this co-operation and lead regulators to seek or strengthen complementary co-operation initiatives beyond the EU.

The UK's request for the OECD to conduct an IRC Review is testament to the country's ambition of ensuring that its IRC processes follow international best practices. It is a unique opportunity for the UK to continue showing leadership on the regulatory policy agenda, in an emerging policy area where most countries are still struggling to establish the basis of the approach. To support the United Kingdom in this endeavour, the OECD provides recommendations and aspirational directions in three areas:

- building a holistic IRC vision, a strategy and political leadership for IRC in the United Kingdom, with clearly defined roles and responsibilities for key players, to develop quality regulation in a globalised context.
- better embedding IRC considerations in policy tools throughout the rulemaking cycle in order to guarantee that they are genuinely and systematically considered by UK departments and regulators;
- increasing awareness and understanding about IRC across departments and regulators, including on the variety of existing IRC practices, and engage stakeholders to inform the development of IRC initiatives.

# Key terms used in the report

**Regulation** is the diverse set of instruments by which governments set requirements on enterprises and citizens. Regulation include all laws, formal and informal orders, subordinate rules, administrative formalities and rules issued by non-governmental or self-regulatory bodies to whom governments have delegated regulatory powers (OECD, 2018[1]).

Although there is no agreed definition of **international standards** across international organisations, the term is used in this report in its "WTO" understanding. The TBT Committee set out six principles for the development of international standards,[1] including i) transparency; ii) openness; iii) impartiality and consensus; iv) effectiveness and relevance; v) coherence; and vi) the development dimension. In addition, WTO case-law provides some guidance.[2] For an instrument to be considered an "international standard" under the TBT Agreement it must both: constitute a "standard" (i.e. a document approved by a recognized body, that provides, for common and repeated use, rules, guidelines or characteristics for products or related processes and production methods, with which compliance is not mandatory) and be "international" in character, i.e. adopted by an international standardising body.

International normative documents developed by international organisations go beyond such international standards. Therefore, to encompass the broader range of legal and policy documents adopted by international organisations, and in line with the approach used in (OECD, 2018[1]), this report refers to the broader term of **international instruments**. These cover legally binding requirements that are meant to be directly binding on member states and non-legally binding instruments that may be given binding value through transposition in domestic legislation or recognition in international legal instruments. This broad notion therefore covers e.g. treaties, legally binding decisions, non-legally binding recommendations, model treaties or laws, declarations and voluntary international standards.[3]

**Better regulation or regulatory policy** is the set of rules, procedures and institutions introduced by government for the express purpose of developing, administering and reviewing regulation. (OECD, 2018[1])

**International regulatory co-operation (IRC)** is defined, following (OECD, 2013[2]), as any agreement or institutional arrangement, formal or informal, between countries to promote some form of coherence in the design, monitoring, enforcement or *ex post* evaluation of regulation. It also includes the unilateral efforts of countries to account for the international environment in domestic rulemaking and the impacts of regulations beyond borders.

The report refers to "**departments and regulators**", be they government departments, executive agencies or non-departmental bodies, to characterise the range of national bodies responsible for making and enforcing regulation. Box 3.1 specifies further the categories of UK bodies with regulatory powers. Some of the better regulation requirements apply specifically to government departments and selected regulatory agencies – it is specified in the review when it is the case.

## References

OECD (2018), *OECD Regulatory Policy Outlook 2018*, OECD Publishing, Paris, https://dx.doi.org/10.1787/9789264303072-en. [1]

OECD (2013), *International Regulatory Co-operation: Addressing Global Challenges*, OECD Publishing, Paris, https://dx.doi.org/10.1787/9789264200463-en. [2]

OECD/WTO (2019), *Facilitating Trade through Regulatory Cooperation: The Case of the WTO's TBT/SPS Agreements and Committees*, OECD Publishing, Paris/World Trade Organization, Geneva, https://dx.doi.org/10.1787/ad3c655f-en. [3]

## Notes

[1] TBT Committee Decision on Principles for the Development of International Standards, Guides and Recommendations with relations to Articles 2, 5 and Annex 3 of the TBT Agreement (G/TBT/1/Rev.13, Annex 2).

[2] For further information see (OECD/WTO, 2019[3]).

[3] For an overview of the different families of international instruments developed by international organisations, ranging from treaties, prescriptive instruments and policy instruments to incentive instruments, technical standards, mutal recognition agreements and supporting instruments, see The Contribution of International Organisations to a Rule-Based International System, 2019, http://www.oecd.org/gov/regulatory-policy/IO-Rule-Based%20System.pdf.

# 1 Context of IRC policies and practices

This chapter documents the context of international regulatory co-operation policies and practices in the United Kingdom. It finds that for now IRC is not yet strongly embedded in the existing institutional and regulatory policy framework. Nevertheless, the United Kingdom has well-established regulatory disciplines, cross government policies providing incentives for a range of regulators to pursue common objectives; and a variety of actors involved in supporting and overseeing the conduct of regulatory policy. This robust Better Regulation Framework puts the United Kingdom in a strong position to make IRC an integral part of the rulemaking process and ensure strong leadership and a strategic whole-of-government vision.

# Regulatory production in the United Kingdom and broad regulatory policy context

The United Kingdom is a strong performer in regulatory policy, with well-established regulatory disciplines, cross government policies providing incentives for a range of regulators to pursue common objectives; and a variety of actors involved in supporting and overseeing the conduct of regulatory policy. This robust Better Regulation Framework puts the United Kingdom in a strong position to take the next step and make the consideration of IRC an integral part of the rulemaking process.

## What regulatory instruments and standards exist in the United Kingdom?

The UK rulemaking system (Box 1.1) distinguishes between primary laws, subordinate regulations (i.e. Statutory instruments, encompassing technical regulations also referred to as "rules"), as well as rulemaking powers bestowed upon regulators through legislation. A significant proportion of these instruments are based on EU law (notably EU Directives and Regulations). In addition, standards (which are mostly used voluntarily by industry to demonstrate performance but can also be the basis of or cited by regulation)[1] are developed through consensus processes at national, European and international level.

---

**Box 1.1. UK Rulemaking: definitions of regulatory instruments and standards**

"Primary legislation is the general term used to describe the main laws passed by the legislative bodies of the United Kingdom, including the UK Parliament."[1]

"Secondary legislation is law created by ministers (or other bodies) under powers given to them by an Act of Parliament (primary legislation). Secondary legislation is also known as 'delegated' or 'subordinate' legislation and often takes the form of a statutory instrument."[2]

Subordinate regulation is most frequently adopted under the form of "Statutory Instruments" drafted by a government department to complement legislative acts. These SIs may take different forms. The most common forms are orders, regulations, rules, and schemes. These statutory instruments encompass technical regulations, also referred to as "rules" (The National Archives, 2017[1]); (House of Commons Information Office, 2008[2]).

In addition, a number of regulatory organisations have specific rulemaking powers bestowed upon them by the UK Parliament e.g. the FCA operates under the Financial Services and Markets Act 2000.

British standards are standards developed and published by BSI,[3] defined as "formal consensus standards as set out in *BS 0:2016 A standard for standards – Principles of standardization* and based on the principles of standardisation policy recognised inter alia in European standardisation policy"[4] as well as by WTO, ISO/IEC (i.e. voluntary process and compliance, consensus, impartiality, openness and balanced participation, transparency, independence and recognition of standards body, fitness for purpose, acceptability, accountability, and coherence).[5]

1 www.parliament.uk/site-information/glossary/primary-legislation/.
2 www.parliament.uk/site-information/glossary/secondary-legislation/.
3 See art. 3.2 BS 0:2016 A standard for standards – Principles of standardization, available at www.bsigroup.com/Documents/30342351.pdf
4 Memorandum of understanding between the United Kingdom Government and the British Standards Institution in Respect of its Activities as the United Kingdom's National Standards Body www.bsigroup.com/globalassets/documents/about-bsi/bsi-uk-nsb-memorandum-of-understanding-uk-en.pdf.
5 Information provided by British Standards Institute.
Source: (The National Archives, 2017[1]); (House of Commons Information Office, 2008[2]); (BSI, 2016[3]).

## Key features of the UK better regulation framework

From the mid-1980s, the United Kingdom has progressively adopted a vigorous and ambitious better regulation agenda, making it a leader in this area (OECD, 2010[4]) and (OECD, 2018[5]). The key principles of the better regulation agenda (transparency, accountability, targeting, consistency and proportionality) were published by the Better Regulation Task Force in 1998 and have been set out in successive reports and policy statements over the years. Also that year, processes for *ex ante* assessment of new regulations were strengthened by the introduction of Regulatory Impact Assessments (RIAs) into the policy making process.

This was followed by the Regulatory Reform Act 2001, which established a fast-track procedure for the amendment of burdensome regulations. The publication of the Hampton Report in 2005 addressed the issues of enforcement and adopting a risk-based approach. The Legislative and Regulatory Reform Act, introduced in 2006, required regulatory bodies to have regard to the better regulation principles when exercising a statutory function. Then the 2008 Regulatory Enforcement and Sanctions Act enacted measures building on the Hampton Report. In addition, the Regulatory Policy Committee (RPC), an advisory non-departmental public body, was established in 2009 to validate departments' estimates of costs and benefits to business. In 2015, the Small Business, Enterprise and Employment Act (SBEE Act) legislated for a Business Impact Target, obliging the Government to set a target for the change of regulatory burdens on business and civil society organisations at the start of each parliament and for the length of it.

The UK Government's better regulation policy is supported by a solid institutional Better Regulation Framework (see Chapter 2 for more detail), a combination of administrative and statutory rules and processes, relying mainly on the Better Regulation Executive (BRE) located in the Department for Business, Energy and Industrial Strategy, as well as the RPC to oversee the system.

This ambitious agenda is reflected in the results of the OECD monitoring of regulatory management tools as displayed in the 2018 Regulatory Policy Outlook (Figure 1.1). The United Kingdom displays the highest composite indicator score for stakeholder engagement for primary laws. Its score for subordinate regulations is also significantly above the OECD average. Stakeholder engagement is required to inform the development of all regulatory proposals, and in practice this is done at both an early and late stage in policy development (OECD, 2018[5]).

### Figure 1.1. United Kingdom Performance on core regulatory management tools

OECD Composite indicators reflecting overall scores on stakeholder engagement, regulatory impact assessment and *ex post* evaluation

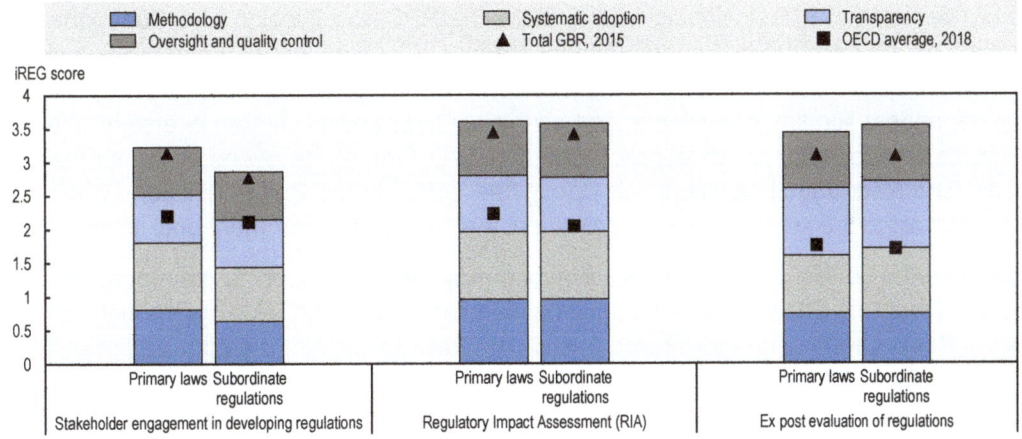

Note: The more regulatory practices as advocated in the OECD Recommendation on Regulatory Policy and Governance a country has implemented, the higher its iREG score.
Source: (OECD, 2018[5]), OECD Regulatory Policy Outlook 2018, Paris, https://dx.doi.org/10.1787/9789264303072-en.

The United Kingdom has also the highest composite indicator score for RIA across the OECD. The United Kingdom has strong formal RIA requirements in place such as: establishing a process to identify how the achievement of the regulation's goals will be evaluated; assessing a broad range of environmental and social impacts; as well as undertaking risk assessments as part of regulatory proposals. The United Kingdom also has a strong triage system in place to ensure that regulatory proposals are subject to proportionate assessment.

The UK composite indicator on *ex post* evaluation is twice the OECD average. There are a range of outlets for affected entities to improve existing laws and regulations; and stakeholders are always consulted when evaluations are conducted.

### *United Kingdom and the European Union to date*

The United Kingdom's former Membership of the EU has consequences both on the domestic rule-making and international co-operation practices. A substantial proportion of UK regulations has originated from the EU, with either direct effect (EU regulations), or requiring transposition into UK legislation (EU directives). Although difficult to evaluate precisely, the UK Government estimates that around 50% of UK legislation with a significant economic impact originates from EU legislation (Miller, 2010[6]).[2]

The domestic work of UK departments and regulators has therefore mainly consisted in adopting EU legislation, regulating areas beyond the EU competence, or implementing regulations (i.e. in enforcement, inspections, market surveillance, etc.). Following withdrawal from the EU, UK departments and regulators are likely to take on additional responsibilities that formerly belonged to European agencies, particularly in the development of new primary and subordinate legislation (National Audit Office, 2017[7]).

At the international level, the EU has competence in several areas in particular those related to trade policy, therefore, until the EU withdrawal, the United Kingdom's international co-operation efforts in this area took place through the intermediary of the EU. In other areas, the United Kingdom was in its own capacity (and sometimes via the EU in addition to its own representation) part of a multiplicity of networks and international organisations with various normative activities.

## Institutional context

### *The main institutions overseeing and conducting IRC*

While not an explicit area of regulatory oversight, a number of governmental bodies have policy supervision functions of relevance to IRC, including mainly BRE, the RPC, the Foreign and Commonwealth Office (FCO), as well as the Department for International Trade (DIT). Oversight of better regulation is provided by BRE, which develops the framework and guidance for better regulation and the RPC, which provides external, independent scrutiny of evidence and analysis. Other bodies with an oversight role include the DIT through its development of trade policy and the FCO through its oversight of international treaty negotiations. The Reducing Regulation Sub-Committee (RRC) in the Prime Minister's Cabinet provided strategic leadership to the better regulation agenda at the centre of government until its abolition in 2019.

Other governmental bodies or external organisations may be called upon to play more *ad hoc* roles in promoting or overseeing IRC activities. This is also the case for the HM Treasury through its Green Book and Magenta Book, OPSS and other bodies outside of Government with a recognised role; including the National Audit Office (NAO) and the United Kingdom Accreditation Service (UKAS). The Government departments, regulatory agencies and British Standards Institution, as the actors developing the regulations or standards, are the critical implementers and infrastructure of IRC, be they within government or outside.

## Figure 1.2. Institutions involved in overseeing and conducting IRC

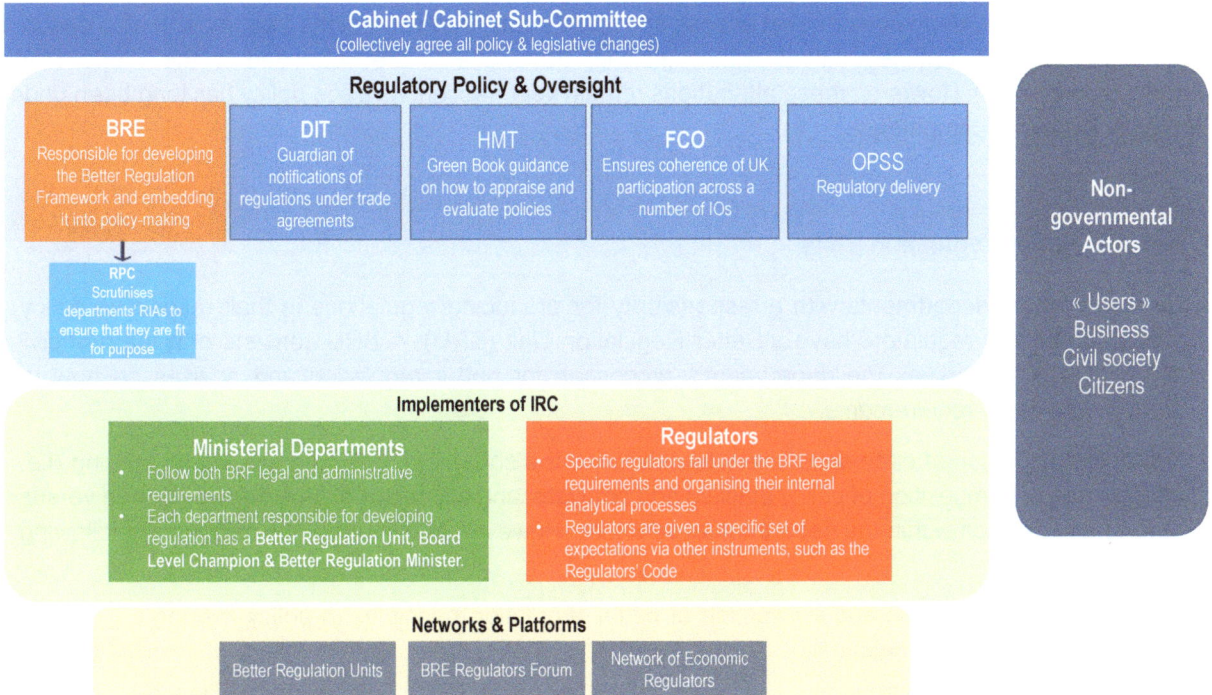

Source: Authors' elaboration.

It is worth noting that devolved administrations can and do have their own better regulation strategies, as illustrated by the examples of the Scottish and Northern Ireland Governments.[3] They therefore have a role to play in incentivising IRC. The report however focuses on the better regulation policies and practices of the United Kingdom. The better regulation and IRC policies of the devolved administrations could be the focus of future OECD work.

The **BRE in the Department for Business, Energy and Industrial Strategy (BEIS)** is responsible for developing the framework and guidance for better regulation and ensuring better regulation disciplines are truly embedded in policy-making. In this context, and even though IRC is not yet an explicit part of better regulation in the United Kingdom, the BRE is well placed to have a general vision on the entry points for IRC in domestic rule-making. It is supplemented by a network of better regulation specialists across departments within **"Better Regulation Units" (BRUs)** that ensure the diffusion of the better regulation agenda (Box 1.2).

The **RPC** is a non-departmental advisory body responsible for providing government departments with external, independent scrutiny of evidence and analysis supporting RIAs of new regulatory proposals and *ex post* evaluations of legislation (OECD, 2018[8]). The RPC also has a complementary statutory role (under the SBEE Act 2015) to scrutinise and verify departments and regulators' assessments of the business impacts of new regulatory measures, that fall within scope of the Business Impact Target. It also undertakes capacity building activities with departments and regulators, through teaching and providing guidance, to improve the evidence base and analysis in their RIAs. Within its activities it has the opportunity to scrutinise the evidence from either foreign or international sources used in both *ex ante* and *ex post* assessments, the estimations of impacts to trade and investment included within the trialled RIA template, as well as the possible relevance of positive/negative externalities of regulatory proposals across the border.

The **DIT** was established in 2016 to develop the United Kingdom's own independent trade policy, and maximise its trade opportunities globally. The Department helps businesses export, drives inward and outward investment, negotiates market access and trade deals, and champions free trade. It also ensures that notifications of draft regulations with significant trade effects are submitted to the World Trade Organization (WTO). However, these attributions remain very nascent as trade policy has long been under the EU's exclusive competence.

> **Box 1.2. Better Regulation Units**
>
> UK Government departments with a responsibility for producing regulations in their respective policy areas and certain regulators have a Better Regulation Unit (BRU). A BRU consists of a team of civil servants which oversees the department's processes for better regulation and advises on how to comply with these requirements.
>
> It is at the discretion of each department to determine the scope of the BRU's role, its resourcing (i.e. staff numbers, composition of policy officials and analysts, and allocation of time on this agenda versus others) and position within the departmental structure. However, BRUs generally perform the following functions:
>
> - Promoting the use and application of better regulation principles in policy making e.g. use of alternatives to regulation.
> - Advising policy teams on how to follow the Better Regulation Framework Guidance processes when developing new regulations.
> - Advising policy teams on how to develop a RIA (or Post-Implementation Review) including queries on methodology and analysis.
> - Advising policy teams on the appropriate time to submit a RIA to the Regulatory Policy Committee for scrutiny.
> - Providing advice to departmental policy teams and regulators on how to meet their SBEE Act obligations regarding reporting against the Business Impact Target (e.g. how to produce assessments of the impacts of new regulatory measures).
>
> BRUs are also responsible for keeping a record of their department's new regulatory provisions, which are then listed in the Government's Better Regulation Annual Report, published by the BRE.
>
> The BRE provides advice and support to BRUs, including running regular "drop-in" sessions where it provides BRU representatives with policy updates and shares examples of best practice.

The **FCO** does not currently have a specific role in overseeing the overall participation of different UK authorities in all IOs of which the United Kingdom is a member, nor does it oversee whether sectoral regulators and/or line ministries have a coherent position across all IOs. It does ensure coherence of UK participation across IOs under FCO responsibility through the activity of permanent delegations. More broadly, the FCO has a potentially important strategic role for IRC, related to the co-operative activities of the United Kingdom: in particular, it sets the UK Government's general strategic plan in terms of foreign policy, and works with international organisations to promote UK interests and global security. The FCO's role in IRC policy may significantly change in the future due to the new "Regulatory Diplomacy" initiative, intended to ensure that the Government has a coherent approach to standards setting and regulation internationally (Box 1.3).

> **Box 1.3. Regulatory diplomacy**
>
> The UK Government has undertaken a cross-departmental "Regulatory Diplomacy" initiative to ensure that the Government has a coherent approach to influencing standards development and regulation internationally. The Regulatory Diplomacy strategy was agreed by the Global Britain Board in Autumn 2018. It comprises three pillars with specific departmental leads: 1) Multilateral & Bilateral Leadership (FCO); 2) Facilitation of Non-State Actors (BEIS); and 3) Trade Policy (DIT). The work is overseen by a cross-government steering group of senior officials, which meets quarterly.
>
> This initiative includes:
>
> - Assessing if the machinery of government is fit for purpose, and reviewing opportunities within existing international fora to increase the United Kingdom's influence;
> - Bringing together policy professionals from across government as well as government partners, including independent regulatory bodies, BSI, and business representative groups, to:
>     - Understand the United Kingdom's priorities in international standards setting and regulation, and the challenges they encounter to influencing internationally;
>     - Share information on respective international-facing activities, and maximise opportunities to influence international rules, standards and policies in line with the United Kingdom's objectives.
> - Co-ordinating a cross-government strategy to enhance UK influence within International Organisations and multilateral fora responsible for standard setting and regulatory co-operation.
>
> These efforts aim to ensure that the United Kingdom's recognised strength in regulation carries the weight that it merits internationally. More broadly, developing the United Kingdom's capacity to engage globally on regulatory matters is expected to support the United Kingdom's cross-cutting international objectives, including improving the global trading environment and supporting the rules-based international system.

Until July 2019, the **Cabinet's Reducing Regulation Sub-Committee** (RRC) gathered Cabinet ministers responsible for overseeing government policy on better regulation, including the principles of good regulation (Box 1.4). Any new regulatory measure, whatever the scale of its impact, required collective agreement and needed clearance from the RRC (in addition to any other relevant Cabinet committees) before it could proceed. The RRC had an active role in driving regulatory initiatives across Whitehall, including the Business Impact Target. Although IRC is not yet an explicit part of better regulation policy, this type of Committee could be well placed at the centre of government to have a strategic overview on the entry points for IRC in domestic rulemaking and to provide strategic leadership to the IRC agenda.

**Better Regulation Board Level Champions** are senior officials supporting Government Ministers. Their role is to ensure that Departmental Board members (the group of senior officials who head the department's main work areas, reporting to the permanent secretary who heads the department) are committed to Better Regulation, provide adequate resources within their departments for it, and liaise with BRE senior management.

> **Box 1.4. Composition of the Reducing Regulation Sub-Committee (RRC)**
>
> The Cabinet and Cabinet Committees are groups of ministers that can take collective decisions that are binding across government. Cabinet Committees reduce the burden on Cabinet by enabling collective decisions to be taken by a smaller group of ministers. The composition and terms of reference of Cabinet Committees are a matter for the Prime Minister but have been stable over the years. They are each supported by a secretariat of Cabinet Office officials.
>
> The RRC, which was abolished in 2019, was responsible for overseeing the Government's policy on better regulation, including the principles of good regulation. Any new regulatory measure, needed clearance from the RRC (in addition to any other relevant Cabinet committees) before it could proceed. The RRC was composed of the following Cabinet Ministers:
>
> - Secretary of State for Business, Energy and Industrial Strategy (Chair)
> - Chancellor of the Duchy of Lancaster and Minister for the Cabinet Office
> - Lord Chancellor, Secretary of State for Justice
> - Secretary of State for International Trade
> - Secretary of State for Environment, Food and Rural Affairs
> - Lord President of the Council, Leader of the House of Commons
> - Chief Secretary to the Treasury
> - Minister of State for Employment
> - Minister of State at the Department for Exiting the European Union
> - Parliamentary Under Secretary of State at the Department for Business, Energy and Industrial Strategy.
>
> Source: www.gov.uk/government/publications/the-cabinet-committees-system-and-list-of-cabinet-committees (accessed 22 October 2019).

**Departments** and **regulators** are the key implementers of IRC activities. UK departments, and certain regulators, have dedicated BRUs (Box 1.2) which oversee the application of better regulation disciplines within their department and co-ordinate with the BRE and RPC in this regard. Departments do not necessarily need to go through central government to carry out their international co-operation activities. Many participate in both European and international bodies, without necessarily consulting with the FCO on their positions. Some UK departments have a specific role in the Better Regulation agenda. They have both a regulatory activity and contribute to the development and/or supervision of regulatory policy. This is the case of OPSS in BEIS for example, and to a lesser extent of the Treasury (through the development of the Green Book).

**The Office for Product Safety and Standards (OPSS)** is a product regulator with responsibility for a range of areas of technical product regulation primarily related to the safety and standards of non-food consumer products, metrology and hallmarking. OPSS is also responsible for the United Kingdom's policy on standards and accreditation, including designating the national standards and accreditation bodies.[4] OPSS works with regulators and businesses to improve regulatory delivery in the United Kingdom. It *"… is the market surveillance or enforcement authority for a wide variety of regulations across the United Kingdom. These include regulations for which BEIS has policy responsibility and regulations where Safety & Standards acts under formal agreements with other Government Departments."* (Office for Product Safety & Standards, 2018[9]). Its attributions on enforcement and conformity assessment give the OPSS an important role in overseeing UK efforts related to regulatory delivery of international agreements, such as Mutual Recognition Agreements (MRAs), and establishing a trustworthy regulatory environment conducive to trade and investment.

Outside of government, a number of bodies contribute and support the functioning of the UK quality infrastructure and regulatory frameworks. **The United Kingdom Accreditation Service (UKAS)** is a not for profit company operating under a MoU with the Government (through BEIS). It is appointed by the UK Government as the sole national accreditation body to assess organisations carrying out conformity assessment activities against internationally recognised standards by the Accreditation Regulations 2009 (SI No 3155/2009) and the EU Regulation (EC) 765/2008. This legal framework sets out that accreditation is performed by the national accreditation body and that conformity assessment bodies seeking accreditation must seek it from the national accreditation body of the Member State in which they are established (i.e. UKAS for bodies established in the United Kingdom). UKAS operates within a European and international accreditation framework through its membership of the European Accreditation Cooperation (EA), the International Accreditation Forum (IAF) and the International Laboratory Accreditation Cooperation (ILAC). UKAS is regularly reviewed by its international peers to demonstrate its competence to operate an accreditation system compatible with the relevant international standards (EA, IAF, ILAC respectively).

The **British Standards Institution (BSI)** is a private company established by Royal Charter. As such, it works under the general authority of BEIS, under the terms set in a MoU between the UK Government and BSI. It develops British standards, enables UK experts' participation in the development of European and international standards, promotes and markets British standards, and supports corporate infrastructure activities to enable the implementation of British standards. In recent years, most British Standards are developed with UK participation in international or European standards bodies.

The **National Audit Office (NAO)** is an independent body that scrutinises public spending on behalf of Parliament. Its key functions include auditing the financial statements of public bodies and a variety of other work including Value-For-Money reports. Whilst the NAO does not have regulatory oversight functions per se, it has played a key role in ensuring the effectiveness of the United Kingdom's Better Regulation agenda, particularly through its previous Value for Money reports into the effectiveness of the Government's Better Regulation policies and processes.[5]

## Existing policy and guidance embedding considerations of IRC

Following a series of relevant milestones reports and policies, the UK Government has produced policy guidance documents as well as a number of major legislative acts setting high-level objectives for departments and regulators, serving as incentives to embed better regulation principles in policymaking and to reduce undue burdens of regulation.

The guidance documents support departments and regulators in applying analytical efforts throughout the regulatory cycle (the Better Regulation Framework, Regulators' Code, HM Treasury Green Book, Enforcement Policies, among others). These tools set an enabling environment for regulators to pursue the effectiveness of regulation, and are thus discussed further in-depth below. So far, however, they remain focused on a largely domestic perspective, and do not very explicitly embed international considerations. Whilst there are references in the HM Treasury Green Book to the importance of gathering evidence from international best practice, IRC does not seem to be directly envisaged as a tool for regulatory effectiveness, and international impacts of regulation (e.g. impacts of regulation on trade) are not part of the key objectives to be pursued by regulators.

However, the Government published in June 2019 a White Paper "Regulation for the Fourth Industrial Revolution" setting out long term plans to enhance its regulatory oversight of technological innovation, including the Government's approach to IRC (Box 1.5). Examples of these reforms include: improving awareness of the effects of regulation on trade among government departments and regulators so that impacts are systematically considered; working with international partners and multilateral fora to develop and promote standards for new and emerging technologies; and including ambitious chapters on good regulatory practices and regulatory co-operation in future free trade agreements.

The relevant UK legislation includes the **Small Business, Enterprise and Employment (SBEE) Act 2015**. It aims to establish a proportionate and efficient better regulation system that focuses on regulations with the greatest potential impact on business and civil society organisations. To do so, it sets out statutory requirements, including for the Government to publish a target for burden reduction, to obtain independent verification of the economic impact of regulatory decisions that count towards that target and for review provisions to be included within secondary legislation (Department for Business, Energy, & Industrial Strategy, 2018[10]). This Business Impact Target reflected the then Government's stated ambition to continue to bear down on the costs of regulation to business while maintaining important regulatory protection. The **Enterprise Act 2016** extended the Business Impact Target to include specified regulators within its scope.

---

### Box 1.5. UK White Paper on "Regulation for the Fourth Industrial Revolution"

The White Paper was published in June 2019, to develop a new agile and flexible approach to regulation in the United Kingdom, a key part of the Government's Industrial Strategy. It sets out a number of reforms to enhance the regulatory oversight of technological innovation, including:

- Establishing a new Regulatory Horizon Council which will advise government on rules and regulations that may need to change to keep pace with technology.
- Piloting an innovation test so that the impact of legislation on innovation is considered during the policy development process.
- Examining the case for expanding the Regulators' Pioneer Fund, which backs projects that are testing new technology in partnership with the regulators in a safe but innovative environment.
- Consulting on a new digital Regulation Navigator to help businesses find their way through the regulatory landscape and bring their ideas to market.
- Asking regulators to go further to evaluate the impact of their initiatives on innovation and consider whether to commence statutory reporting requirements for regulators on the impact of the economic growth duty.
- Seeking to include ambitious chapters on good regulatory practices and regulatory co-operation in future free trade agreements.
- Improving awareness of the effects of regulation on trade among government departments and regulators.

The White Paper initiatives will be delivered overseen by a Ministerial Working Group on Future Regulation, a cross-government group of Cabinet-level Ministers which aims to identify and drive reform in areas of the economy where regulation needs to adapt to support emerging technologies.

Source: www.gov.uk/government/publications/regulation-for-the-fourth-industrial-revolution.

---

The **Deregulation Act 2015** sets a Growth Duty applicable across the UK Government, according to which "any person exercising a regulatory function must have regard to the desirability of promoting economic growth." In particular, in virtue of this growth duty, regulators are to exercise regulatory function "…in a way which ensures that (a) regulatory action is taken only when it is needed, and (b) any action taken is proportionate." (Section 108, Deregulation Act, 2015), and this from the setting of policy to the securing compliance with or enforcement of the regulatory requirements. Additional information on how regulators can work in accordance with the Growth Duty was set out in a statutory guidance document issued in March 2017 (Department for Business, Energy & Industrial Strategy, 2017[11]).

The **Enterprise Act 2016**, in addition to bringing regulators within scope of the Business Impact Target, also requires regulators in scope to publish annual performance reports on the effect of the Growth Duty and the Regulators Code on the way they exercised their functions (Legislation.gov.uk, 2016[12]). These requirements need to be brought into effect by secondary legislation, which has not taken place at the time of writing. However, the government's June 2019 White Paper "Regulation for the Fourth Industrial Revolution" states that the Government wishes to consider whether to commence statutory reporting requirements for regulators on the impact of the economic growth duty.[6]

The major applicable IRC-related legal act when the UK was a Member of the EU was the **UK European Communities Act 1972**,[7] which set the general framework for the effects of the EU legislation in the United Kingdom. In particular, the 1972 Act provided that any EU treaty or legislation resulting from EU treaties "…are without further enactment to be given legal effect or used in the United Kingdom shall be recognised and available in law, and be enforced, allowed and followed accordingly."[8] This encompasses also any international agreements concluded by the EU, and in particular trade agreements.[9] However, under the EU Withdrawal Act 2018,[10] the European Communities Act was repealed upon the UK leaving the EU on 31 January 2020.

The **Constitutional Reform and Governance Act 2010** sets broader requirements on the procedure to follow for other Treaties, beyond those of the European Union. In particular, it provides that all treaties signed by the United Kingdom which are subject to ratification (or its equivalent), or to which the United Kingdom intends to become a party by accession, are to be laid before Parliament. Beyond this, there is no central guidance underpinning UK negotiation and adoption of international instruments and participation in international organisations.

## References

BSI (2016), *A standard for standards - Principles of standardization*, https://www.bsigroup.com/Documents/30342351.pdf. [3]

Department for Business, Energy & Industrial Strategy (2017), *Growth Duty: Statutory Guidance*, https://assets.publishing.service.gov.uk/government/uploads/system/uploads/attachment_data/file/603743/growth-duty-statutory-guidance.pdf (accessed on 22 October 2019). [11]

Department for Business, Energy, & Industrial Strategy (2018), *Business Impact Target: Final report for the 2015-17 Parliament*, https://assets.publishing.service.gov.uk/government/uploads/system/uploads/attachment_data/file/709156/business-impact-target-bit-final-report-2015-2017.pdf. [10]

House of Commons Information Office (2008), *Factsheet on Statutory Instruments*, https://www.parliament.uk/documents/commons-information-office/l07.pdf. [2]

Legislation.gov.uk (2016), *Enterprise Act 2016: Chapter 12*, http://www.legislation.gov.uk/ukpga/2016/12/pdfs/ukpga_20160012_en.pdf. [12]

Miller, V. (2010), *How much legislation comes from Europe?*, House of Commons Library, https://researchbriefings.parliament.uk/ResearchBriefing/Summary/RP10-62 (accessed on 18 February 2019). [6]

National Audit Office (2017), *A Short Guide to Regulation*, https://www.nao.org.uk/wp-content/uploads/2017/09/A-Short-Guide-to-Regulation.pdf. [7]

OECD (2018), *Case Studies of RegWatchEurope Regulatory Oversight bodies and the European Union Regulatory Scrutiny Board*, OECD, Paris, http://www.oecd.org/gov/regulatory-policy/regulatory-oversight-bodies-2018.htm (accessed on 3 March 2019). [8]

OECD (2018), *OECD Regulatory Policy Outlook 2018*, OECD Publishing, Paris, https://dx.doi.org/10.1787/9789264303072-en. [5]

OECD (2010), *Better Regulation in Europe: United Kingdom 2010*, Better Regulation in Europe, OECD Publishing, Paris, https://dx.doi.org/10.1787/9789264084490-en. [4]

Office for Product Safety & Standards (2018), *What you can expect of Safety and Standards Enforcement*, https://www.gov.uk/guidance/national-regulation-enforcement-services (accessed on 14 February 2019). [9]

The National Archives (2017), *Statutory Instrument Practice*, http://www.legislation.gov.uk/pdfs/StatutoryInstrumentPractice_5th_Edition.pdf. [1]

## Notes

[1] BSI estimates that some 15% of BSI standards including European and international standards are cited in regulation. (Standards Outlook, BSI 2018: https://content.yudu.com/web/43fqt/0A43ghs/IssueOneNovember2018/html/index.html).

[2] Estimating the precise share of UK legislation coming from Europe is challenging. Research by the House of Commons Library estimated the share of statutory instruments implementing EU Directives over 2010-2013 to 9.4%. However, once EU regulations (of direct application) are taken into account, the total share reached 59% for the same years. Given the shortcomings of both calculations, the House of Commons Library concluded that "it is possible to justify any measure between 15% and 55%". https://commonslibrary.parliament.uk/brexit/the-eu/how-much-legislation-comes-from-europe/.

[3] www.gov.scot/policies/supporting-business/business-regulation/ and www.economy-ni.gov.uk/articles/better-regulation.

[4] www.gov.uk/government/organisations/office-for-product-safety-and-standards/about.

[5] www.nao.org.uk/report/the-business-impact-target-cutting-the-cost-of-regulation/.

[6] www.gov.uk/government/publications/regulation-for-the-fourth-industrial-revolution.

[7] www.legislation.gov.uk/ukpga/1972/68/contents.

[8] Art. 2 para. 1 UK European Communities Act 1972.

[9] Ibid. Art. 1 paras 2, 3 and 4.

[10] www.legislation.gov.uk/ukpga/2018/16/section/1/enacted.

# 2 Embedding the international environment in the rule-making machinery

This chapter presents the various entry points for departments and regulators to embed international considerations in their domestic rulemaking. It finds that IRC is implicit rather than explicit in the UK Better Regulation Framework and related regulatory policy tools and disciplines, resulting in case by case IRC practices by departments and regulators. To a certain extent, IRC is promoted from a trade facilitation perspective: through the consideration of international standards and the introduction of a trade question in a new regulatory impact assessment template. In addition, the experience with the EU framework may prove useful to embed international considerations more widely and the well-established system of regulatory oversight can be used to introduce cross-cutting IRC considerations.

The UK regulatory process offers several entry points for departments and regulators to embed international considerations in their domestic rulemaking. Prior to the EU withdrawal there was strong anchorage to EU legislation since accession in 1973 (strong UK presence and role in EU institutions). In addition, references to the international context exist throughout the UK better regulation disciplines:

- international instruments and overseas practices may be considered in the context of identifying different alternatives to address a specific policy challenge;
- a new RIA template is being trialled, with a trade and investment-related question, introducing a new entry point for consideration of international impacts of regulation;
- post-implementation reviews may be used to identify how a domestic measure's impact compares to different approaches followed abroad.

There is ample room to strengthen the consideration of international and foreign expertise and rules in the United Kingdom's Better Regulation Framework. Beyond the EU framework, these existing avenues for unilateral IRC remain mostly case-by-case, depending on the subject matter and departments and regulators' willingness. The inclusion of trade and investment questions in the impact assessment template is still at its beginning. It is therefore too early to assess its effectiveness. The United Kingdom is still considering the methodology and guidance for measuring the trade impact at the time of writing.

The well-established system of regulatory oversight enables the streamlining of broad governmental objectives throughout regulatory processes in the United Kingdom. However, the Better Regulation Framework and RPC scrutiny and guidance currently incentivise departments to focus primarily on the Business Impact Target. Going forward, this solid infrastructure could be used to introduce cross-cutting IRC considerations.

## Scope of better regulation in the United Kingdom: domestic focus, with European considerations

### *Better Regulation Framework*

The Better Regulation Framework Guidance (latest update, August 2018), produced by the Better Regulation Executive, sets out the scope of application and the processes that Government officials should follow when developing new regulatory measures. In terms of scope, it frames both a broad range of regulatory measures included and a strong focus on business or voluntary and community bodies. The Better Regulation Framework Guidance applies to all regulatory measures, defined as measures that regulate business activity (the full definition of what constitutes "regulatory provision" is set out in Section 22 of the SBEE Act). This encompasses both primary legislation as well as statutory instruments (i.e. secondary legislation)[1] and even non-legislative measures that regulate business activity.

In terms of bodies (Box 2.1), the Framework mainly applies to government departments (regulatory agencies may follow their own processes and may be incentivised/ given a specific set of expectations via other instruments, such as the Regulators' Code as outlined below). More precisely, the Framework includes both legal and administrative requirements:

- The *legal requirements* apply to both government departments *and specified regulatory bodies* under the provisions of the SBEE Act 2015 and Enterprise Act 2016.[2] These include the requirement for departments and regulators to submit assessments of the economic impact of new regulatory provisions (that fall within the scope of the Business Impact Target) to the RPC for independent verification.
- The *administrative requirements* apply to government departments (the other independent regulatory bodies are responsible for organising their own internal analytical processes). These are rules that have been collectively agreed within government which stipulate the need for officials to

develop RIAs to support effective policy making and to meet the needs of collective decision making and stakeholder engagement, including Parliamentary scrutiny. These administrative requirements include the HM Treasury Green Book guidance[3] on how to appraise and evaluate policies, projects and programmes, and the Cabinet Office Guide for Making Legislation.[4]

> **Box 2.1. Types of regulatory bodies in the United Kingdom**
>
> National regulatory bodies in the United Kingdom vary in their legal status, structure, powers and lines of accountability. They are responsible for putting government policy in practice. They can be broadly broken down into 4 categories: Government departments; non-ministerial departments; executive agencies and non-departmental public bodies:
>
> - Core departmental functions are an integral part of a department, headed by a Minister and staffed by civil servants.
> - Non-Ministerial Departments (NMDs) are headed by senior civil servants and not ministers. Their staff are civil servants. They usually have a regulatory or inspection function. The Food Standards Agency is an example. Some of the economic regulators (Ofgem which regulates the gas and electricity sectors, and Ofwat, which regulates water services) are NMDs.
> - Executive Agencies are part of government departments and usually provide government services rather than decide policy – which is done by the department that oversees the agency. The parent department minister is ultimately responsible for their work. The department is responsible for funding and ensuring good governance. Unless explicitly created by statute, they can be reformed without primary legislation. An example is the Driver and Vehicle Licensing Agency (overseen by the Department for Transport).
> - Non-Departmental Public Bodies (NDPBs) are not part of a department, and carry out their functions at arms-length from government. They have varying degrees of independence but are directly accountable to ministers. NDPBs tend to be set up through statute, and most need primary legislation to alter their institutional framework. There are four types of NDPBs, two of which may have regulatory functions: 1) Executive NDPBs work for the government in specific areas, for example, the Environment Agency; 2) Advisory NDPBs provide independent, expert advice to ministers – for example, the Committee on Standards in Public Life.
>
> Regulatory bodies range from large bodies with a wide range of powers, like the Environment Agency, to smaller, highly specialised regulators, like the Adventure Activities Licensing Authority. Some national regulators have direct rule-making powers, whereas others do not. They may have joint enforcement responsibilities with local authorities in some of their regulatory responsibilities. Five major national regulatory bodies – the Health and Safety Executive (HSE), Environment Agency, Food Standards Agency, Competition and Markets Authority and Financial Conduct Authority – are responsible for regulating areas such as health and safety at work, financial services, environment regulation, competition and consumer protection, food hygiene and safety.
>
> Source: Based on (OECD, 2010[1]), Better Regulation in Europe: United Kingdom, Paris, https://dx.doi.org/10.1787/9789264084490-en and www.gov.uk/government/how-government-works.

Based on the SBEE Act, Figure 2.1 gives a general flowchart on the regulatory provisions that fall under the scope of UK Better Regulation Framework Guidance, and as such under the scrutiny of the UK Regulatory Policy Committee.

Figure 2.2 gives an overview of the successive phases of Better Regulation in the United Kingdom. IRC considerations may intervene at three moments of this better regulation framework:

- in Stage 1, when departments develop policy options and conduct an impact assessment;
- in Stage 2, when departments conduct public consultations, and, in parallel to the UK Better Regulation framework, when they notify drafts to the EU and the WTO; and
- in Stage 3, in the context of post-implementation reviews.

### Figure 2.1. Regulatory measures under the scope of UK Better Regulation

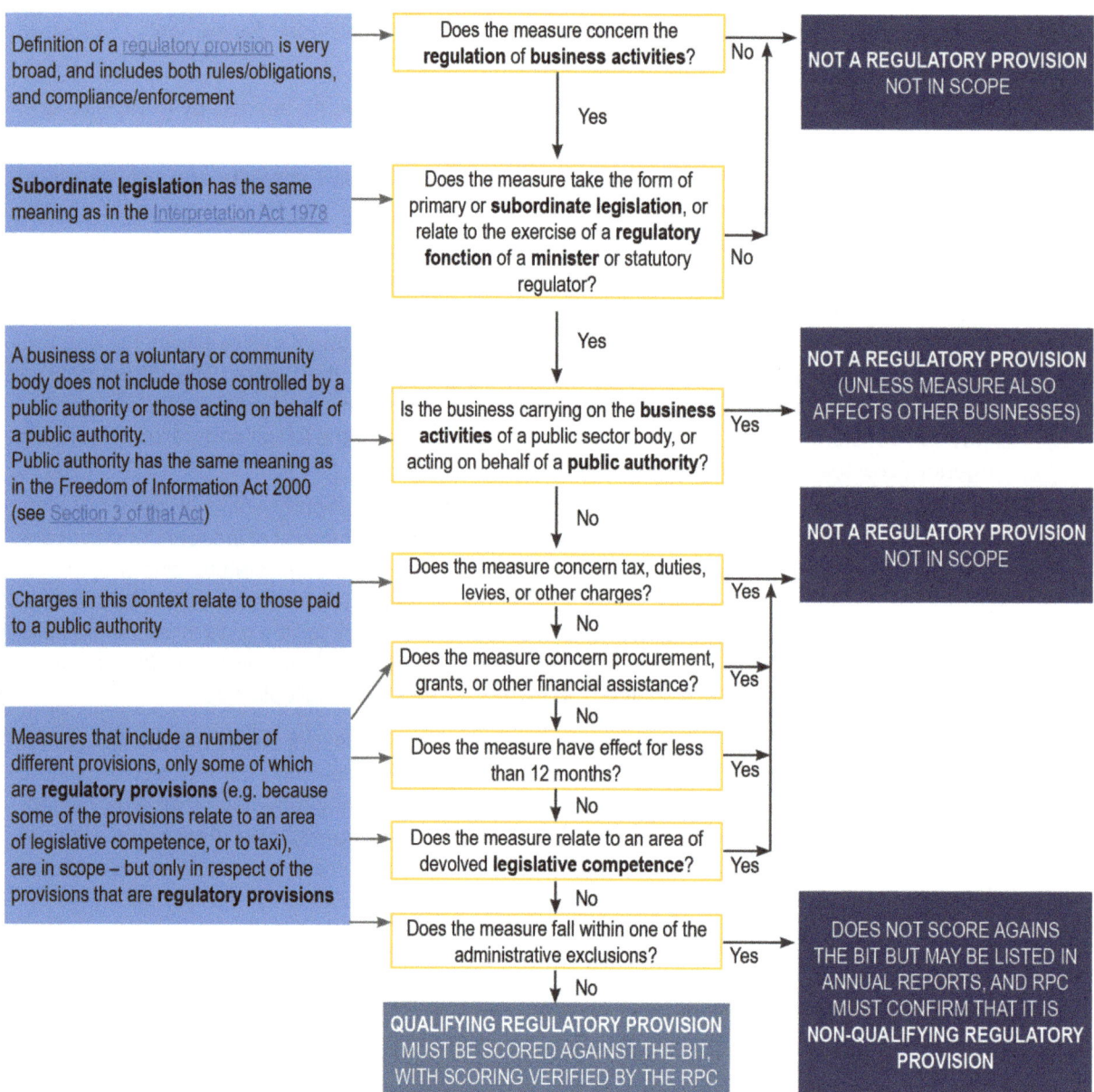

Note: The terms in bold have specific meanings set out in the SBEE Act 2015, http://www.legislation.gov.uk/ukpga/2015/26/contents/enacted.
Source: (OECD, 2018[2]), Figure 8.1.

## Figure 2.2. Better regulation phases in the United Kingdom

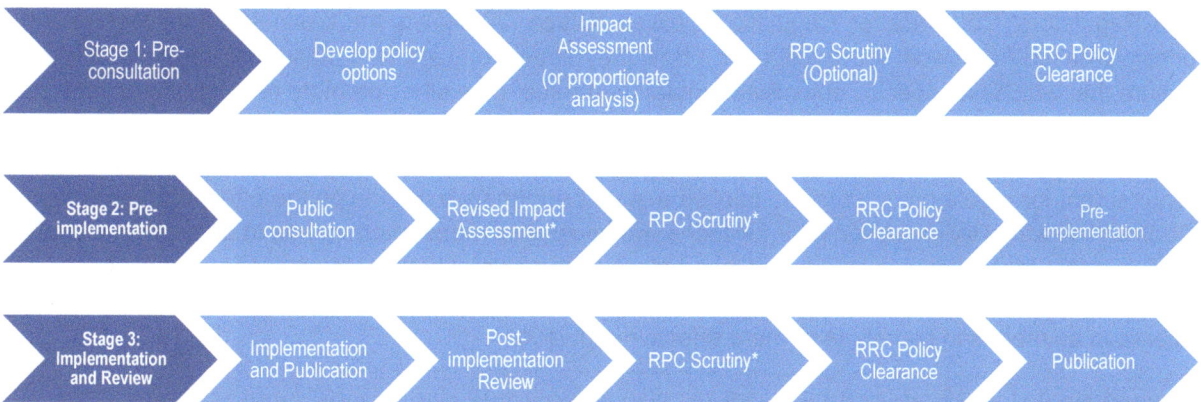

* At this stage a full RIA and RPC scrutiny is optional only for measures below the threshold of ± GBP 5m EANDCB and those measures that are certified as being within the administrative exclusions categories.
Source: Better Regulation Framework, Department for Business, Energy and Industrial Strategy, August 2018.

To ensure greater proportionality in the Better Regulation Framework, a new "de minimis rule" has been introduced to the Framework. It gives Departments greater flexibility to determine the appropriate level of analysis to demonstrate the rationale for a regulation, along with its impacts and benefits that meets the needs of Parliament and stakeholders. The BRE and the RPC have jointly produced guidance (Regulatory Policy Committee, 2019[3]) for departments and regulators on estimating the proportionality of regulatory proposals.

The rule stipulates that at the pre-implementation and review stages (Figure 2.2) only measures with *significant* regulatory impacts (greater than -/+ 5m GBP threshold)[5] are expected to have full RIAs and be submitted to the RPC for scrutiny. However, some measures that fall below the de minimis threshold may still be expected to produce a full RIA if they are estimated to have significant distributional impacts; disproportionate burdens on small businesses; significant wider social, environmental, financial or economic impacts; or significant novel or contentious elements.

All other regulatory measures are still expected to produce a proportionate level of analysis to support stakeholder and parliamentary scrutiny of the proposal. In addition, the framework guidance states that departmental Chief Analysts are responsible for ensuring that the analysis used for a measure which is under the -/+ 5 m GBP threshold is sufficiently robust. Other scrutiny opportunities in the policy making process involve the interdepartmental collective agreement process and parliamentary scrutiny.

The Better Regulation Framework Guidance states that measures that do not fall under the definition of a "regulatory provision" under the SBEE Act are excluded from the scope of the BIT (e.g. fees or charges, measures with no impact on business). It also lists a number of additional "administrative exclusions". These are rules that the Government has collectively agreed to remove from the scope of the BIT e.g. regulatory provisions related to incorporation of EU law and other international commitments and obligations (except where such measures go beyond what is required by EU/international rules, i.e. "gold plating") or implementation of the EU Withdrawal Agreement.

In addition to the Better Regulation Framework Guidance, supplementary guidance documents assist departments and regulators in applying Better Regulation disciplines to their rulemaking processes, including Statutory Guidance for Regulators on implementing the Business Impact Target (Department for Business, Energy & Industrial Strategy, 2019[4]) and Best Practice Principles for Post-implementation reviews (Department for Business, Energy & Industrial Strategy, 2018[5]).

### Regulators' Code

The Regulators' Code (Better Regulation Delivery Office, 2014[6]) is the basic statutory text setting a principle-based framework for regulators on how they should engage with those they regulate. It aims to ensure that whichever specific objectives regulators pursue, they all "…promote proportionate, consistent and targeted regulatory activity through the development of transparent and effective dialogue and understanding between regulators and those they regulate."[6] The Enterprise Act 2016 introduced a requirement for regulators in scope to publish annual performance reports on the effect of the Regulators Code on the way they exercised their functions. However, this requirement needs to be brought into effect by secondary legislation, which has not taken place at the time of writing. In any case, this Code remains a purely domestic tool, without references to cross-border impacts of regulation or international co-operation as means to contribute to more effective regulation.

## International considerations within regulatory impact assessments (RIA)

The RIA framework provides an iterative process whereby departments are obliged to reflect on alternative options, to consider how other jurisdictions are addressing similar challenges (particularly relevant for new areas of regulation), to map the existence of international legal instruments and policy standards in the same field (OECD, 2017[7]) and to consider the cross-border implications of new regulations. It should also be an iterative process, where individual steps can be reassessed as new information comes to light. RIAs may also increase the attention of policy makers for the trade impacts of new regulatory measures and thus ensure a conscious balancing of trade and other public policy considerations.

Although the HM Treasury Green Book points to the importance of gathering evidence from international best practice, the UK RIA process is in practice largely focused on domestic evidence and considerations. Nevertheless, a number of entry points in the different steps of the RIA process do allow for the consideration of the international environment, namely in the rationale and policy options for proposed regulations, and in the actual assessment of impacts of regulatory drafts.

### International considerations as part of rationale and policy options for proposed regulations

UK departments and regulators initiating action to address a specific policy challenge should launch a ROAMEF (Rationale, Objectives, Appraisal, Monitoring, Evaluation and Feedback) cycle, described in the *Green Book: Central Government Guidance on Appraisal and Evaluation*. The first step of this cycle is to describe a rationale for government intervention, to generate a long list of possible options to achieve the objectives, and to narrow the list down to a short list suitable for a detailed cost benefit analysis. This list of options is included within the RIA template.

There are very few formal requirements to consider the international environment at this stage (although the HM Treasury Green Book does point to the importance of gathering evidence from international best practice).[7] However, international normative instruments or best practices can contribute to the rationale of the measure, and are indeed used on a case-by-case basis to justify regulations. For example, the Department for Environment, Food, and Rural Affairs (Defra) introduced a law prohibiting the purchase and sale of ivory. To justify this regulation, Defra referred to existing international conventions and rules, and responses in other countries (to the problem under consideration). Defra also mentioned externalities impacting upon Africa from the United Kingdom's trade in ivory in the rationale for intervention and the United Kingdom's global leadership in the global movement to end trade of ivory (in the policy objectives and intended effects).[8]

As part of its scrutiny of RIAs, when the RPC is aware of evidence that has not been taken into account, it can question and make reference to it. This is therefore an opportunity to introduce evidence from foreign or international sources (although the RPC does not always have knowledge of such evidence itself) and to consider the impacts of regulatory divergence. In practice, the RPC mostly prompts departments to introduce international considerations by asking whether such evidence exists.

### Trial trade and investment questions in impact assessment procedures

A new RIA template was issued in 2018, including a new question related to the impacts of UK regulations on international trade and investment (i.e. *Is this measure likely to impact on trade and investment? Yes/No*). In the previous template, the only related question with a clear international focus, aimed to identify regulatory proposals going beyond EU requirements. Through the new question, departments are required to consider more generally the international impacts of the policies they are developing. As part of the overall approach, it helps to ensure that the UK policy-making processes remain compliant with the country's WTO Agreements. When fully implemented, the new question will place the United Kingdom among the OECD countries using their RIA process to consider regulatory impacts on trade (OECD, 2018[8]) and, potentially, linking the notification and the impact assessment processes (OECD, 2018[9]).

DIT and BRE have produced guidance to help policymakers answer the trade question. The guidance aims to support policymakers in estimating the impact of the regulatory policy they are drafting may have on international trade or investment into, and out of, the United Kingdom. The guidance complements the RIA template with additional questions for departments' consideration, namely to help them identify the impacts their draft will have on export, import, value of trade and investment, discrimination. These questions remain broad, calling for yes / no answers, without requiring an estimate of the quantified impact. Where policy makers answer "yes", they are asked to provide "a couple of lines outlining the rationale and a qualitative assessment of the rationale". DIT, BRE and the RPC are currently considering how to refine the methodologies to support departments in measuring the trade impacts of their draft measures.

Given the recent introduction of the questions, the RPC has had very little opportunity to scrutinise departments' assessment of trade or investment impacts. . Of the 69 impact assessments submitted by UK Departments to the RPC during the pilot phase of the new template (January – November 2019), 30 used the template which included the new trade question. Of those, 8 answered 'yes', suggesting an impact on trade and investment, 14 answered no, 2 answered n/a, and 6 left the question uncompleted.

The new trade and investment RIA has allowed to identify draft regulations that created directly or indirectly impacts on trade and/or investment due to new product safety standards, alterations to product design, new labelling requirements and increased bureaucratic procedures (not present in other countries). The RPC scrutiny revealed that the departments estimating that there was no trade or investment impact or that such impact was minimal were correct in their estimations. Among the departments that did not answer the trade and investment question, the RPC identified some that had missed trade and investment impacts. In such cases, the RPC co-ordinated with the DIT to conduct extra analysis and advise the departments in revising their assessment. Overall, following the pilot phase the RPC identified a need for more and better quality guidance and training to departments to assist them in considering trade and investment impact, as well as engagement of BRE and DIT senior management across government to ensure top-down support for a more systematic consideration of trade and investment impacts in departments' conduct of RIAs. Overall, the pilot phase was useful to engage with departments on trade and investment and highlight priorities for a better implementation of the new template.

## Consideration of international instruments

Beyond the WTO requirements to align national regulation with international standards[9] and the spontaneous practices of a number of departments and regulators, there is no specific UK statutory obligation to consider, or broader incentives to be consistent with, international instruments in rulemaking. The Better Regulation Framework nevertheless encourages the use of standards as a basis for regulation, insofar as the use of standards via non-regulatory means is exempted from the scope of the Business Impact Target.[10] Given the strong alignment of British standards to international and European standards, this provides for an important (although indirect) channel to promote the embedding of international standards in domestic rulemaking.

The standards system in the United Kingdom is a single national standard model, where a single standard is sought for any given issue. It is the role of BSI, as the National Standards Body of the United Kingdom, to develop British Standards with consideration to European and international standards. While the United Kingdom was a member of the EU, there was an obligation for BSI to adopt all European standards (ENs) developed by CEN, CENELEC and ETSI, as well as to withdraw existing British standards that conflict with such European standards (BSI, 2019[10]). All international standards from ISO and IEC are adopted as British Standards unless the national committee considers that they are of little or no value to the UK economy. Consequently, of the current 37 000 British standards, 82% have been developed through European or international processes with UK expert participation. There are increasingly fewer standards that are developed "British only" Figure 2.3.

### Figure 2.3. International references in BSI standards

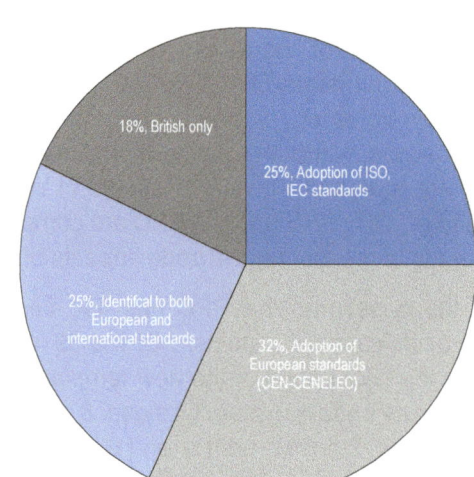

Source: Information provided by BSI, December 2018.

Beyond the incentives provided by the WTO requirements for the harmonisation of technical regulation through the adoption of international standards, different departments and regulators have also seen the intrinsic value of adopting international instruments more broadly in their respective area (although this is done with limited sharing of experience and practices across sectors). This is the case for instance of the UK Office for Nuclear Regulation (ONR), which relies strongly on the International Atomic Energy Agency (IAEA) to underpin its approach to safety, in particular the IAEA safety standards programme involving some 200 safety standards developed over 50 years. The ONR considers these standards based on international consensus as the cornerstone of the global nuclear safety regime (see the related case study in Chapter 4). They are seen as a robust framework of fundamental principles, requirements and guidance to ensure safety, applicable, as relevant, throughout the entire lifetime of facilities and activities.

## Stakeholder engagement

The United Kingdom has a well-established domestic framework to engage with stakeholders, deeply rooted in a tradition of general public consultations. Anyone can respond to the consultations, including foreign stakeholders. However, there is no specific procedure to target and engage with foreign stakeholders.

In addition, the United Kingdom has notification obligations that open a period of comment before the draft is adopted in which foreign governments and stakeholders may comment. In particular, the UK had notification obligations to the EC while it was still a member of the EU. In addition, it has notification obligations to the WTO.

### General framework for stakeholder engagement

The UK public consultation framework is based on flexible guidance, rather than statutory obligations, currently embodied by Consultation Principles updated in 2018 to provide for a proportionate and targeted approach (Box 2.2) (UK Cabinet Office, 2018[11]). Overall, consultations tend to be conducted for all primary laws and subordinate regulations in the United Kingdom.

The UK consultation policies and practices are largely focused on domestic stakeholders. Principle F of the UK Consultation Principles, requiring consultations to be targeted to specific groups, allows for an avenue for regulators to target specific foreign stakeholder groups that may be affected. Still, while not banning their contribution, the Consultation Principles do not promote explicitly the participation of foreign stakeholders or the specific needs for adapted consultation processes when appropriate.

---

**Box 2.2. United Kingdom Consultation Principles 2018**

The UK Cabinet Office adopted a set of principles in 2012 (updated in 2018) to guide government officials across Whitehall in their efforts to conduct public consultations. These Principles cover the following:

A. Consultations should be clear and concise
B. Consultations should have a purpose
C. Consultations should be informative
D. Consultations are only part of a process of engagement
E. Consultations should last for a proportionate amount of time
F. Consultations should be targeted
G. Consultations should take account of the groups being consulted
H. Consultations should be agreed before publication
I. Consultations should facilitate scrutiny
J. Government responses to consultations should be published in a timely fashion
K. Consultation exercises should not generally be launched during local or national election periods.

Source: (UK Cabinet Office, 2018[11]), Consultation Principles,
https://assets.publishing.service.gov.uk/government/uploads/system/uploads/attachment_data/file/691383/Consultation_Principles__1_.pdf.

---

### Notifications of domestic regulatory drafts

Notification procedures to international *fora* can be an opportunity to gather evidence on cross-border impacts of regulations, as well as to gain additional evidence from foreign peers or stakeholders. In particular, notifications of technical barriers to trade (TBT) and of sanitary and phytosanitary (SPS) measures are a well-established discipline that span both the EU and international level. The United Kingdom submits notifications of draft regulations to the World Trade Organization (WTO) and as an EU member did so also to the European Commission (EC). As of March 2020, the authorities responsible for WTO notifications are the Department for International Trade (DIT) for TBT and the Department for Environment Food and Rural Affairs (Defra), via the EC, for SPS measures.

*Notifications of measures to the European Commission*

EU members notify to the EU Commission draft technical regulations on goods and on information society services that have a significant impact on trade, allowing them to gain feedback on these measures from other EU members (Box 2.3). While still a member of the EU, the United Kingdom was an active user of the EC notification mechanism. In 2018, the United Kingdom submitted 33 notifications to the EC, situating it in the higher average of EU notifying countries well above the EU average of 24 notifications. To these notifications, the United Kingdom received only one comment from the EC, out of a total of 96 comments issued over the year to all EU members, and another one from a member state.[11]

The UK Government prepared guidelines to assist regulators in submitting notifications to the EC (Department for Business Innovation and Skills, 2016[12]). A decision tree developed by the UK Government was provided to help policymakers determine whether a measure needed to be notified (Department for Business Innovation and Skills, 2016[13]). There was no additional criterion of the expected impact of the measure on the Single Market, but notifying bodies were required to annex the impact assessment to the notification.

This EC notification process was also the opportunity for the United Kingdom to identify proposals of other EU member states that may affect UK interests and/or the effectiveness of the Single Market. Each relevant lead department was required to review notifications available on the Technical Regulation Information System. To provide meaningful comments, the notification guidelines required them to consult with key stakeholders from government, business associations or trade associations, as appropriate (Department for Business Innovation and Skills, 2016[12]).

---

**Box 2.3. Notification of technical regulations to the European Commission by EU member States**

All EU member States notify the EC, and through it all other EU and EFTA member states, about draft technical regulations on goods and on information society services that have a significant impact on trade. After notifying a draft regulation member states are required to leave a "standstill period" of at least 3 months before adopting the said regulation.[1] During this standstill period, the EC and other member states may raise concerns about potential barriers to trade created by the notified draft regulation. In particular, they may raise "comments", which are not binding but must be considered by member states, or a "detailed opinion" if they consider that the measure may represent an obstacle to the free movement of goods or the freedom to provide information society services. In the case of a detailed opinion, member states must take it into account and reply to it, explaining the actions it intends to take in response.

Notifications by all EU member states are made via the EC's Technical Regulations Information System, and all member states have designated a contact point within their government to ensure that notifications and comments are centralised by this authority. Lack of notification to the EU renders the measure unenforceable. In other words, national courts or other enforcement authorities will not have the right to enforce the regulation despite its entry into force (Department for Business Innovation and Skills, 2016[13]).

1 These obligations result from Directive (EU) 2015/1535 of the European Parliament and of the Council of 9 September 2015 laying down a procedure for the provision of information in the field of technical regulations and of rules on Information Society services (Text with EEA relevance) https://eur-lex.europa.eu/legal-content/en/txt/?uri=celex%3a32015l1535.

*Notification of measures to the WTO*

The scope of the WTO obligation goes beyond the EU and results in information on draft UK regulations shared with all 164 members of the WTO. It includes notification obligations in a range of Agreements concerning trade in goods as well as trade in services, namely under the WTO Agreements on the Application of Sanitary and Phytosanitary Measures (SPS Agreement), and of Technical Barriers to Trade (TBT Agreement), as well as the General Agreement on Trade in Services (GATS). The scope of measures to be notified under the SPS and TBT Agreements is similar to those of the EC notifications: technical regulations, conformity assessment procedures as well as sanitary and phytosanitary measures, regardless of their legal nature.

However, the WTO agreements set additional requirements not included in the EC notification process that relate to the potential impacts of draft measures. They require for instance that WTO members notify to other members the draft mandatory regulations that may have a significant effect on trade and are not based on international standards. In addition, both the SPS and TBT Committees encourage WTO members to notify measures even when they are based on international standards (WTO, 2009[14]) (WTO, 2008[15]). This notification should be done at an early appropriate stage, when amendments can still be introduced and comments taken into account.[12] Given the notification is a legal obligation for WTO members, lack of notifications to the WTO may result in a formal dispute in front of the WTO dispute settlement body.

Once draft measures are notified to the WTO, the WTO Secretariat makes these drafts publically accessible on its website, and provides the contact details of the enquiry points of all WTO members.[13] As a result, the United Kingdom may receive comments not only from other WTO members but also any interested stakeholders, whether public or private.

Under the EU Common Commercial Policy, the EC submits notifications to the WTO in respect of draft EU legislation on behalf of all member states. As an EU member, the United Kingdom used to submit notifications of draft national legislation (except for SPS[14]), which fell outside of the scope of EU responsibility, if it considered that these had a significant effect on trade and deviated from international standards. In effect, in line with most EU member states, the United Kingdom submitted very few notifications to the WTO in comparison to other non-EU developed countries. In 2018, the United Kingdom submitted four TBT notifications to the WTO and no SPS notifications to the WTO. They included measures adopted by devolved administrations (Northern Ireland, Scotland, Wales), and transition measures after withdrawal from the EU.[15] Looking ahead, after the withdrawal from the EU the UK will no longer have measures falling under EU responsibility. It will be directly responsible for notifying to the WTO in all fields and its volume of notifications may therefore grow closer to the level of other non-EU developed countries.

## Post-implementation reviews

*Ex post* reviews can provide a critical opportunity to identify the potential divergence with international frameworks as well as the trade and other IRC impacts of laws and regulations (Basedow and Kauffmann, 2016[16]). These tools complete the RIA process by allowing deeper insights into the impacts of a regulatory measure (via feedback from affected parties and de facto implementation) and can help build the evidence on IRC throughout the rule-making cycle.

In the United Kingdom, under the provisions of the SBEE Act, Government departments are required to include a statutory review clause in new secondary legislation that is estimated to have significant impacts on business. The inclusion of a review clause (or an equivalent administrative commitment to carry out a review) then requires policy officials to undertake a Post-Implementation Review (PIR).[16] In addition, HMT have produced a Magenta Book (HM Treasury, 2011[17]) (to be considered alongside the HMT Green

Book), which provides departments with methodological guidance on how policies and projects should be assessed and reviewed.

A PIR seeks to establish whether and to what extent, the regulation has achieved its original objectives; has objectives that remain appropriate; is still required and remains the best option for achieving those objectives; and could be achieved in another way, which involves less onerous regulatory provisions. The BRE provides a template to help regulators in the conduct of PIRs. It is non-mandatory but provides a useful guide as to the sorts of questions departments should be attempting to address (Box 2.4). Whilst this template does not include a requirement to measure unintended impacts of the regulation for foreign stakeholders or deviation from international instruments, it directs departments to identify how the United Kingdom's implementation of EU measures compares with other EU member states (see point G in Box 2.3).

In light of the findings from the PIR, officials are expected to advise their respective minister with information on whether the measure should be retained without changes, amended, repealed or replaced. PIRs for measures with a review clause must be published alongside the relevant regulations.[17] Normally PIRs are completed within five years of the regulatory measure coming into force and on a repeated five-year cycle thereafter. However, the RPC has noted a shortfall in the numbers of PIRs carried out by departments in the last 2015-17 Parliament: "of the 80 expected during the 2015-17 parliament, the RPC has received 43".[18]

Reviews for UK measures implementing international instruments may be conducted but are not carried out systematically (although the RPC has recommended that their undertaking would depend on the nature of the instrument and on the legislation implementing it). The *OECD Regulatory Policy Outlook 2018* (OECD, 2018[8]) finds that *ex post* evaluation related to IRC is relatively nascent for most OECD countries, although data shows some progress since 2014. For example, almost three times as many countries indicate having completed an assessment of consistency with comparable international instruments as part of *ex post* reviews in the last 12 years than were reported in 2014 (from 3 to 8). However, this represents only a subset of OECD countries – around one in five.

---

### Box 2.4. Post Implementation Review Template

The BRE have provided a template to guide departments on how to set out the findings of a PIR. Its use is not mandatory but recommended. The questions are as follows:

A. What were the policy objectives of the measure?
B. What evidence has informed the PIR?
C. To what extent have the policy objectives been achieved?
D. What were the original assumptions?
E. Were there any unintended consequences?
F. Has the evidence identified any opportunities for reducing the burden on business?
G. For EU measures, how does the UK's implementation compare with that in other EU member states in terms of costs to business?

Source: (Department for Business, Energy & Industrial Strategy, 2018[5]), Producing post-implementation reviews: principles of best practice, www.gov.uk/government/publications/business-regulation-producing-post-implementation-reviews.

# Regulatory delivery

The delivery phase of laws and regulations is a critical and often overlooked area of regulatory policy. The best designed laws and regulations will fail if the infrastructure for their proper implementation is weak, notably the compliance and enforcement mechanisms. It is also an area where co-operation and consideration for the international environment may help significantly reduce costs and burdens for the regulated entities and improve the effectiveness of the regulatory measures. For example, co-ordination with foreign authorities may be essential to avoid regulatory arbitrage or to effectively manage regulated activities with strong cross-border spillovers.

Conformity assessment procedures allow companies to demonstrate compliance with regulatory requirements. They are a key component to facilitate international trade and avoid unnecessary costs both for exporting and importing goods and services. As an EU member, the United Kingdom benefitted from a robust framework for recognition of UK conformity assessment results both by other EU members and beyond (via mutual recognition agreements concluded by the EU).

Enforcement policies present important opportunities for embedding considerations for the international environment and co-operation with peers from other jurisdictions. As an EU member, the United Kingdom relied strongly on domestic enforcement and on the relevant networks and mechanisms provided by the EU (for example the EU rapid alert system for dangerous non-food products – see the case study on product safety in Chapter 4). These networks of regulators are explored in Chapter 4. This section investigates some existing sectoral enforcement policies and their consideration of IRC.

## *Conformity assessment, accreditation*

*What is conformity assessment and accreditation and what are they used for?*

Conformity assessment is the demonstration that a product, process, service, system, person or body meets specified requirements (e.g. testing, calibration, inspection and certification).[19] These requirements may be found in a regulation (most often within technical regulations), a national or an international standard. Prior to importing a product or service, conformity assessment procedures (CAPs) allow a business or manufacturer to demonstrate that they comply with any regulatory requirements and /or have addressed any legitimate end-user concerns so that their product is therefore safe to import to the market of destination (OECD, 2017[7]). Dependent on risk, conformity assessment may range from 'internal production control' (self-assessment) to third party conformity assessment by accredited bodies.

The bodies or organisations performing these activities are collectively known as conformity assessment bodies (CABs). Accreditation is the process whereby the technical competence, impartiality and integrity of CABs is assessed and evaluated, usually against the requirements of international standards, e.g. ISO17065.[20] Therefore an assessment performed by accredited CABs provides the public and government confidence that standards are being met.

Accredited third party conformity assessment necessarily entails costs for businesses. To comply with various regulatory regimes, exporting UK businesses may need to undergo different or duplicative CAPs in their home market and in the market of destination. These can be costly and burdensome to businesses, hindering access to markets and export opportunities. Discussions in the WTO show that divergent conformity assessment procedures are perceived as an even higher impediment to trade than divergent regulations (Karttunen and McDaniels, 2016[18]). Acknowledging this, the World Trade Organization (WTO) Agreement on Technical Barriers to Trade strongly encourages countries to recognise the results of other countries' conformity assessments. Common regulatory framework (such as provided by the EU) and international standards (through the International Laboratory Accreditation Cooperation – ILAC – and the International Accreditation Forum – IAF) provide bases for alignment in conformity assessment and accreditation.

As a member of the EU, the United Kingdom followed the European legislative framework on conformity assessment and accreditation.[21] The EA MLA provides the European market with a network of CABs that are competent within their scope of accreditation to issue reliable and credible statements of conformity for products and services, thereby reducing costs and adding value to business and consumers. The UK Government supports this conformity assessment framework through its Conformity Assessment and Accreditation policy which sets out the high level principles and guidance on conformity assessment and accreditation in the United Kingdom including the importance of considering accreditation against existing European and international regulatory approaches and standards (BEIS, 2017[19]).

*EU legal and institutional framework for conformity assessment procedures (CAPs)*

The EU legislation provides a comprehensive framework for conformity assessment that applies throughout EU member states.[22] As an EU member, UK businesses benefitted from the equivalent arrangements in all other EU countries and from the mutual recognition of their own CA results at the EU level. The framework includes in particular:

- A range and level of CAPs for the EC, Council, and the European Parliament to use depending on different circumstances. These include product type and complexity and the level of risk from non-conformity (art. 4, Decision 768/2008). To ensure a common approach to each different CAPs, the EU Decision 768/2008 provides standard texts of CAPs including definitions and general obligations for economic operators that can be adopted as such by member states.
- An obligation for all CABs carrying out procedures set out in EU legislation to be notified to the EC, which holds a database of all CABs operating in EU member countries. This same obligation applies to EU member states, EFTA countries (EEA members) and other countries with which the EC has concluded Mutual Recognition Agreements (MRAs) and Protocols to the Europe Agreements on Conformity Assessment and Acceptance of Industrial Products (PECAs).
- A single National Accreditation Body per country, undertaking accreditation in their respective territories. This body operates in the public interest and run as a non-profit organisation.[23]

*UK Framework on conformity assessment procedures and accreditation*

Through the conformity assessment and accreditation policy principles, the United Kingdom encourages UK CAPs to be consistent with European and international standards. CABs are also required to use the CIPM MRA as the reference point for measurement standards.

Member states notify the Commission and the other member states the bodies, fulfilling the relevant requirements, designated to carry out conformity assessment according to specific EU legislation. Both the notification of Notified Bodies and their withdrawal are the responsibility of the notifying member state. While it was a member of the EU, the United Kingdom notified 177 conformity assessment bodies to the EC, that were listed in the NANDO (New Approach Notified and Designated Organisations) Information System, the EU database.[24] As of the withdrawal date, "UK notified bodies will be removed from the Commission's information system on notified organisations (NANDO database). As such, UK bodies will not be in a position to perform conformity assessment tasks pursuant to Union product legislation as from the withdrawal date."[25]

The UK Government is currently establishing a domestic legal framework to enable UK CABs to continue operating for most products placed on the UK market after the UK withdrawal from the EU. Under this framework, UK CABs recognised by the EU will be converted into UK Approved Bodies (or UK-recognised RTPO, UI or TAB respectively) so that they can continue to carry out compliance processes for the UK market.[26] It is expected that the UK product safety framework mirrors the existing EU framework as far as possible and the technical requirements for becoming a UK Approved or recognised Body will be broadly the same as the current EU requirements.

In line with the EU Regulation, the United Kingdom has designated UKAS as the sole accreditation body. Accreditation remains voluntary, but is strongly encouraged. Like for conformity assessment, BEIS has developed additional guidance principles in complement to the EU framework on accreditation. UKAS has recognition at the European level, from the European co-operation for Accreditation (EA),[27] and at the international level, from the ILAC and the IAF. UKAS' participation in EA allows to ensure accreditation Europe-wide, and its accreditation by ILAC-IAF provides it additional recognition beyond the EU. Prior to withdrawal, as part of a EU member country, UKAS participated in ILAC-IAF through the intermediary of EA who acts on behalf of all member states.

Outside of relevant EU regulatory requirements UKAS accreditation will still be recognised and accreditation certificates will continue to be valid. The UK Government has confirmed that UKAS' role as the sole national accreditation body including for most UK conformity assessment bodies will continue.

### *Enforcement*

The Regulators' Code directs all regulators to have an enforcement policy available. A number of regulators have made their enforcement policy statement available on line. This is the case for example of the Health and Safety Executive[28] and of the Office for Nuclear Regulation (ONR, 2019[20]). While most enforcement policies focus purely on the domestic level, they offer an opportunity for greater consideration of the international environment.

As an illustration, the Enforcement Policy developed by OPSS in Spring 2017 (Department for Business, Energy & Industrial Strategy, 2018[21]) and updated in 2018, sets out the principles for dealing with non-compliance with product regulation. While mostly focusing on enforcement of regulations within the domestic borders, the Enforcement Policy applies in an international context so far as non-compliance presents risks beyond the border. In cases where non-compliance presents a risk beyond the United Kingdom, namely in EU member states, OPSS is meant to co-ordinate with foreign counterparts. Art 5.6 of the Enforcement Policy, applicable in the transition period, provides that:

> *"Where we identify non-compliances which result in products being seized, recalled, withdrawn from sale, or removed from the market, and we consider that the non-compliances present a risk beyond the United Kingdom, we will make a referral under the European Union (EU) "safeguarding provisions" to our counterparts in other EU Member States and to the European Commission."*

The FCA's Approach to Enforcement (FCA, 2019[22]) paper sets out how international co-operation and collaboration forms part of the FCA's enforcement work. It explains how they work with international regulators and law enforcement agencies, to share information and intelligence, and to detect and take action to tackle cross-border misconduct. It further sets out how international co-operation is important in helping to identify how criminal proceeds might be laundered through the United Kingdom's financial markets.

The withdrawal from the EU heightens the risk of weakening the market surveillance and enforcement capacities of UK departments and regulators in a number of sectors – this is well illustrated by both the case study on product safety and that on medical products in Chapter 4. This is an area where significant co-operation efforts are needed to maintain the effectiveness of regulation, all the more that digitalisation and new technologies raise new enforcement threats with the dematerialisation of transactions. In this context, it is not surprising that OPSS's 2018-2020 Strategy highlights the importance of IRC to address global safety risks, build a trustworthy system for consumers, and reduce costs to business (see the case study on product safety in Chapter 4).

## References

Basedow, R. and C. Kauffmann (2016), "International Trade and Good Regulatory Practices: Assessing The Trade Impacts of Regulation", *OECD Regulatory Policy Working Papers*, No. 4, OECD Publishing, Paris, https://dx.doi.org/10.1787/5jlv59hdgtf5-en. [16]

BEIS (2017), *Conformity assessment and accreditation policy*, https://www.gov.uk/government/publications/conformity-assessment-and-accreditation-policy-the-uks-quality-infrastructure (accessed on 5 March 2019). [19]

Better Regulation Delivery Office (2014), *Regulators' Code*, http://www.legislation.gov.uk/ukpga/2006/51/pdfs/ukpga_20060051_en.pdf. [6]

BSI (2019), *How are standards made?*, https://www.bsigroup.com/en-GB/standards/Information-about-standards/how-are-standards-made/. [10]

Department for Business Innovation and Skills (2016), *Decision Tree to determine whether a measure requires notification*, https://assets.publishing.service.gov.uk/government/uploads/system/uploads/attachment_data/file/510161/BIS-16-151-Directive-2015-1535-EU-decision-tree-to-determine-whether-a-measure-requires-a-notification.pdf. [13]

Department for Business Innovation and Skills (2016), *Directive 2015/1535/EU Guidance for Officials*, https://assets.publishing.service.gov.uk/government/uploads/system/uploads/attachment_data/file/490271/BIS-16-15-directive-2015-1535-guidance.pdf. [12]

Department for Business, Energy & Industrial Strategy (2019), *Business Impact Target Statutory Guidance*, https://assets.publishing.service.gov.uk/government/uploads/system/uploads/attachment_data/file/776507/Busines__Impact_Target_Statutory__Guidance_January_2019.pdf. [4]

Department for Business, Energy & Industrial Strategy (2018), *Producing Post-Implementation Reviews (PIR): Principles of best practice*, https://assets.publishing.service.gov.uk/government/uploads/system/uploads/attachment_data/file/726992/producing-post-implementation-reviews-pir.pdf. [5]

Department for Business, Energy & Industrial Strategy (2018), *Safety and Standards Enforcement: Enforcement Policy*, https://www.gov.uk/guidance/national-regulation-enforcement-services. [21]

Department for Business, E. (2017), *Small Business, Enterprise and Employment Act 2015*, https://assets.publishing.service.gov.uk/government/uploads/system/uploads/attachment_data/file/674755/small-business-act-s31-statutory-review-requirements.pdf (accessed on 23 October 2019). [25]

FCA (2019), *FCA Mission: Approach to Enforcement*, https://www.fca.org.uk/publication/corporate/our-approach-enforcement-final-report-feedback-statement.pdf. [22]

HM Treasury (2011), *The Magenta Book: Guidance for evaluation*, https://assets.publishing.service.gov.uk/government/uploads/system/uploads/attachment_data/file/220542/magenta_book_combined.pdf. [17]

Karttunen, M. and D. McDaniels (2016), "Trade, Testing and Toasters: Conformity Assessment Procedures and the TBT Committee", *Journal of World Trade*, Vol. 50/3. [18]

OECD (2018), *Case Studies of RegWatchEurope Regulatory Oversight bodies and the European Union Regulatory Scrutiny Board*, OECD, Paris, http://www.oecd.org/gov/regulatory-policy/regulatory-oversight-bodies-2018.htm (accessed on 3 March 2019). [2]

OECD (2018), *OECD Regulatory Policy Outlook 2018*, OECD Publishing, Paris, https://dx.doi.org/10.1787/9789264303072-en. [8]

OECD (2018), *Review of International Regulatory Co-operation of Mexico*, OECD Publishing, Paris, https://dx.doi.org/10.1787/9789264305748-en. [9]

OECD (2017), *International Regulatory Co-operation and Trade: Understanding the Trade Costs of Regulatory Divergence and the Remedies*, OECD Publishing, Paris, https://dx.doi.org/10.1787/9789264275942-en. [7]

OECD (2010), *Better Regulation in Europe: United Kingdom 2010*, Better Regulation in Europe, OECD Publishing, Paris, https://dx.doi.org/10.1787/9789264084490-en. [1]

OECD/WTO (2019), *Facilitating Trade through Regulatory Cooperation: The Case of the WTO's TBT/SPS Agreements and Committees*, OECD Publishing, Paris/World Trade Organization, Geneva, https://dx.doi.org/10.1787/ad3c655f-en. [23]

ONR (2019), *ONR Enforcement Policy Statement*, http://www.onr.org.uk/documents/enforcement-policy-statement.pdf. [20]

Regulatory Policy Committee (2019), *Proportionality guidance for departments and regulators*, https://assets.publishing.service.gov.uk/government/uploads/system/uploads/attachment_data/file/800603/Final_proportionality_.pdf. [3]

UK Cabinet Office (2018), *Consultation Principles*, https://assets.publishing.service.gov.uk/government/uploads/system/uploads/attachment_data/file/691383/Consultation_Principles__1_.pdf. [11]

WTO (2009), *Fifth Triennial Review of the Operation and Implementation of the Agreement on Technical Barriers to Trade Under Article 15.4. G/TBT/26.*. [14]

WTO (2008), *Recommended Procedures for Implementing the Transparency Obligations of the SPS Agreement (Article 7), G/SPS/7/Rev.2.*. [15]

WTO (2003), *The EC Notification Authority and Enquiry Point for the WTO Agreement on the Application of Sanitary and Phytosanitary Measures: Operational Procedures and Recent Experience*. [24]

## Notes

[1] https://assets.publishing.service.gov.uk/government/uploads/system/uploads/attachment_data/file/735587/better-regulation-framework-guidance-2018.pdf.

[2] The list of 52 relevant regulators that fall within scope of the Business Impact Target, is set out in *the Business Impact Target (Relevant Regulators) Regulations 2017*. This list includes regulators that are *"legally separate entities to UK Ministers and carry out functions that regulate business and/or the voluntary and community sector"*. In the vast majority of cases these will be bodies that are established under statute. However, given the wide array of regulatory bodies, this category also includes a small number of bodies that have been established either as a company or by Royal Charter rather than by statute.

[3] www.gov.uk/government/publications/the-green-book-appraisal-and-evaluation-in-central-governent.

[4] https://assets.publishing.service.gov.uk/government/uploads/system/uploads/attachment_data/file/645652/guide_to_making_legislation_jul_2017.pdf.

[5] The government's primary metric to assess progress against the Business Impact Target is the Equivalent Annual Net Direct Cost to Business (EANDCB). This is a measure of the direct impact of a regulatory decision on business, where a direct impact is defined as an impact that can be identified as resulting directly from the implementation or removal/simplification of the regulation.

[6] See Foreword of Regulators' Code (Better Regulation Delivery Office, 2014[6]).

[7] References in the Green Book to international evidence:

> **Para 2.7** "Generating a long-list of options at the start of the appraisal process ensures that a full range of possibilities are considered. This should be informed by stakeholder consultation or engagement, lessons learned from previous interventions, ***international best practice*** and the wider evidence base. Starting out with a narrow set of options or a pre-determined solution may miss the opportunity to explore more novel, innovative solutions that might offer better social value." (emphasis added)
>
> **Para 3.7** "Analysis and assumptions should have an objective basis in research. Relevant evidence can be drawn from evaluations of past interventions, evidence of "what works", ***international comparisons***, academic and other literature and relevant experience. The strategic dimension should also identify where there are gaps in the evidence base." (emphasis added)
>
> **Para 4.16** "Where appropriate evaluations of previous or similar interventions, ***international*** and wellbeing evidence, should be used to design options that build on what works, to avoid repeating past mistakes. Box 6 provides an example of the use of evaluation evidence and piloting. This is particularly important when considering the scope of a proposal and the service solution (the technical means of delivering the intervention). When assessing the relevance of previous evaluation, allowance should be made for differences in context, circumstances and culture." (emphasis added)
>
> **A3.14** "A ***review of international evidence*** provides an estimate of the marginal utility of income at 1.3.36 This is used by DWP in distributional analysis. The estimate of the marginal utility of income can be used to calculate welfare weights to adjust costs and benefits."

⁸ See https://assets.publishing.service.gov.uk/government/uploads/system/uploads/attachment_data/file/710369/ivory-bill-ia.pdf, Decision 17.70 et seq. of Decisions of the Conference of the Parties to CITES in effect after the 17th meeting, http://www.cites.org/eng/dec/index.php.

⁹ In particular, the World Trade Organization's (WTO) Agreements on Technical Barriers to Trade (TBT) and on the Application of Sanitary and Phytosanitary Measures (SPS): i) require the use of international standards as a basis for national regulations in certain situations, ii) require justification if international standards are not used (including through science-based risk assessments in the SPS area), iii) incentivise members to fully harmonise measures with international standards, and iv) strongly encourage members to participate in the development of international standards. See (OECD/WTO, 2019[23]).

¹⁰ See Better Regulation Framework, Annex 1.

¹¹ http://ec.europa.eu/internal_market/scoreboard/performance_by_governance_tool/tris/index_en.htm.

¹² See Art. 2.9 TBT Agreement; Annex B para. 5 SPS Agreement.

¹³ See TBT Information Management System http://tbtims.wto.org/; and SPS Information Management system http://spsims.wto.org/.

¹⁴ See further clarification on the EU notification procedure for the SPS Agreement in (WTO, 2003[24]) and for the TBT Agreement at https://www.wto.org/english/tratop_e/tbt_e/8_EU_EP_e.pdf.

¹⁵ G/TBT/N/GBR/31.

¹⁶ Guidance is available for regulators to decide whether or not to include a review provision (Department for Business, 2017[25]).

¹⁷ www.legislation.gov.uk.

18
https://assets.publishing.service.gov.uk/government/uploads/system/uploads/attachment_data/file/720816/regulatory_overview_2015-17_parliament_final_pdf.pdf.

¹⁹ See article 2, Regulation (EC) No 765/2008, https://eur-lex.europa.eu/lexuriserv/lexuriserv.do?uri=oj:l:2008:218:0030:0047:en:pdf. See also in this regard ISO/IEC 17000:2004, Conformity assessment — Vocabulary and general principles, which defines conformity assessment as: "demonstration that specified requirements relating to a product, process, system, person or body are fulfilled" (art. 2.1). An explanatory note elaborates: 'Note 1 The subject field of conformity assessment includes activities defined elsewhere in this International Standard, such as testing (4.2), inspection and certification, as well as the accreditation of conformity assessment bodies", https://www.iso.org/obp/ui/#iso:std:iso-iec:17000:ed-1:v1:en.

²⁰ E.g. ISO/IEC 17065, 17020, 17021, 17024, 17025 or according to Regulation (EC) No 765/2008.

²¹ Regulation (EC) No 765/2008 of the European Parliament and of the Council of 9 July 2008 setting out the requirements for accreditation and market surveillance relating to the marketing of products, https://eur-lex.europa.eu/lexuriserv/lexuriserv.do?uri=oj:l:2008:218:0030:0047:en:pdflex.europa.eu/lexuriserv/lexuriserv.do?uri=oj:l:2008:218:0030:0047:en:pdf.

²² http://ec.europa.eu/DocsRoom/documents/18027/attachments/1/translations.

[23] Regulation (EC) No 765/2008, https://eur-lex.europa.eu/lexuriserv/lexuriserv.do?uri=oj:l:2008:218:0030:0047:en:pdf.

[24] http://ec.europa.eu/growth/tools-databases/nando/index.cfm?fuseaction=country.notifiedbody&cou_id=826.

[25] https://ec.europa.eu/info/sites/info/files/file_import/industrial_products_en_1.pdf.

[26] https://www.gov.uk/guidance/status-of-conformity-assessment-bodies-after-brexit#the-new-uk-legal-framework

[27] UKAS will maintain its membership in EA for 2 years as of 31 January 2020.

[28] HSE, Enforcement Policy Statement, www.hse.gov.uk/enforce/enforcepolicy.htm (accessed 23 October 2019).

# 3 Regulatory co-operation practices and tools

This chapters gives an overview of the bilateral, regional and multilateral co-operative efforts of the United Kingdom on regulatory matters. These take various forms, including through Memoranda of Understanding (MoUs), treaties, mutual recognition agreements (MRAs), trade agreements, or participation in regional or multilateral fora. The United Kingdom has notably traditionally been very active in international fora in various sectors and policy areas. Its co-operation efforts have been very much shaped by its former membership in the EU and its ties with Commonwealth countries. This chapter identifies opportunities to encourage a more consistent approach to international regulatory co-operation across Whitehall and further maximise the benefits of UK regulators co-operation activities.

The United Kingdom has traditionally been active internationally in various co-operation fora on regulatory matters, including on regulatory policy, in various sectors and policy areas, as well as in both the design and the delivery of regulation. External co-operation efforts of UK departments and regulators have so far been largely influenced by the UK membership of the EU. UK co-operation beyond the EU has also been shaped by historic relations with Commonwealth countries or cultural ties, although this and the co-operation partners largely depend on the sector.

Membership in a number of European agencies and networks have enabled UK departments and regulators to shape regulatory approaches at the EU level and to participate in exchange of information and evidence. As of February 2020, UK's participation in various EU agencies, bodies and networks remains pending confirmation until the end of the "transition period" prior to the taking effect of any "future economic partnership" still to be negotiated between the EU and the United Kingdom by the end of 2020, and may depend on each different agency / body / network. According to the Withdrawal Agreement,[1] the United Kingdom will no longer be represented in EU institutions, bodies, offices and agencies, but EU law will still apply in the United Kingdom during this transition period.

While the United Kingdom was a member of the EU, trade policy fell under the Common Commercial Policy, an exclusive competence of the EU. The majority of UK co-operation agreements, whether in the form of trade agreements or mutual recognition agreements (MRAs) were negotiated through the intermediary of the EU. With its withdrawal from the EU, the United Kingdom has started defining its own trade policy and strategy for negotiations of trade agreements and MRAs. With variations among sectors, the United Kingdom is also seeking new bilateral partnerships with other countries, and further engagement at the global level. International agreements mostly take the form of treaties and Memoranda of Understanding (MoU). The United Kingdom is also strengthening its technical assistance capacity in various sectors.

Competence in some sectors, for example financial services, did nevertheless remain to an extent at the member state level. For instance, in October 2018, the UK's Financial Conduct Authority concluded a Mutual Recognition of Funds (MRF) with the Securities and Futures Commission (SFC) of Hong Kong concerning Covered Funds, Covered Management Companies and regulatory co-operation.[2] Other bilateral agreements are reported in the case study on financial services in Chapter 4.

The United Kingdom has traditionally been active in international rulemaking, beyond the EU. It has been a founding member of several major IOs. Its membership in most IOs is not likely to be impacted by a withdrawal from the EU, with the exception of certain organisations where the United Kingdom's participation used to take place through the intermediary of the EU. It is likely that the United Kingdom will invest even further in these multilateral *fora* after withdrawal from the EU. Indeed, one of the key objectives of the FCO's foreign policy, as embodied in the regulatory diplomacy initiative (Box 1.3), is to project UK influence worldwide, while strengthening the rule-based international system and promoting UK interests and values. Beyond influence, participation in international regulatory networks comes critically in support of effective regulatory delivery as highlighted in the case studies developed in Chapter 4.

## The traditional UK international co-operation instruments: treaties and Memoranda of Understanding

The United Kingdom can conclude international agreements with other States, creating binding obligations under international law, or Memoranda of Understanding (MoUs) which express intentions but not binding commitments (Foreign and Commonwealth Office, 2014[1]). The development of such international agreements is decentralised, but the FCO plays an important role in ensuring that the binding commitments are consistent with UK obligations and publically disclosed.

Any UK government department may lead negotiations of an international treaty, but the responsibility for concluding treaties involving the United Kingdom lies with the Secretary of State for Foreign and Commonwealth Affairs. The FCO reviews all draft treaties, and is responsible for overseeing the policy aspects of treaties as well as the form used and procedure followed to ensure that the negotiated text conforms with both UK and international law.

As a dualist state, after ratification of treaties by the Government, the Parliament needs to incorporate the text of the treaty into national law by legislation.[3] This is true for any binding agreement, including trade agreements. Until withdrawal from the EU, the only exception were EU Treaties and Regulations that used to be considered incorporated into UK law and binding at the domestic level without the need for a further act of Parliament (UK European Communities Act 1972).

MoUs are more flexible than treaties and can be negotiated and concluded by any government department or regulator. The procedure to develop MoUs is less formal, and the FCO does not scrutinize draft MoUs before their finalisation. Typically, MoUs may be concluded on subject matters that may evolve and require frequent changes, or to facilitate procedures of exchange of information directly between the United Kingdom and foreign authorities. For example, the UK Financial Conduct Authority (FCA) has concluded MoUs with many of its regulatory counterparts, which facilitate the exchange of information and support investigative assistance related to the supervision and oversight of regulated entities in the United Kingdom and the partner jurisdiction. Examples include MoUs signed between the FCA and the Hong Kong Securities and Futures Commission (SFC)[4], the United States Commodity Futures Trading Commission (CFTC),[5] and the Reserve Bank of India[6] (see the case study on financial services in Chapter 4). The United Kingdom has also established many MoUs to support the exchange of confidential information with countries beyond the EU in relation to medical products (see the case study on medical and healthcare products in Chapter 4).

As a result of its oversight functions, the UK FCO keeps track of international agreements concluded between the United Kingdom, whether by central government or sectoral authorities, and foreign authorities. Its database is used to provide information to departments asking about international commitments, to public enquiries and to feed into UK Treaties Online (UKTO), an online search facility.[7] It does not disclose all agreements however. In particular, MoUs concluded by Departments other than the FCO for example are not systematically listed.

## Exchange of information and technical assistance

UK departments and regulators exchange information frequently with peers in different countries, whether at the European level – until recently mostly facilitated by common participation in European regulatory agencies, networks and bodies – or with other foreign partners, often facilitated by cultural or historic ties, for example via the Commonwealth. For example, the Office for Nuclear Regulation (ONR), in support of its core regulatory purposes, proactively works with international regulatory bodies to co-ordinate positions and engagement and exchange regulatory and technical information, experience and expertise on nuclear safety and security. This includes formal agreements such as Nuclear Cooperation Agreements (NCAs) and Information Exchange Arrangements (IEAs). The ONR has developed a strategic engagement framework that stands out in its mapping of relevant partners and in its vision of international co-operation, including a definition of the regulator's international footprint (Chapter 4).

In addition, many UK regulators play an active role in sharing their experience with regulators from other countries in order to build capacity abroad. As an example, ONR commits to working with aspirant nuclear nations to support the development of high standards of safety and security. The global nature of the nuclear industry and the potential trans-boundary impact of any severe nuclear accident means it has a role to play in raising the bar internationally for public protection and to learn lessons for the United Kingdom on how to improve its regulatory regime. The OPSS also maintains a Technical Assistance

Programme, which provides technical advice to developing countries in order to promote the reform or design of regulations, laws and strategies (Chapter 4).

## The building of new co-operation capacities: trade and mutual recognition agreements

The major UK trading partner is the EU, accounting for 49.5% of its imports and exports. Major non-EU partners include the United States, China and Russia (Figure 3.1, and Figure 3.2).

### Figure 3.1. United Kingdom: exports to and imports from main partner countries

As a per cent of total gross and value added exports and imports, 2015

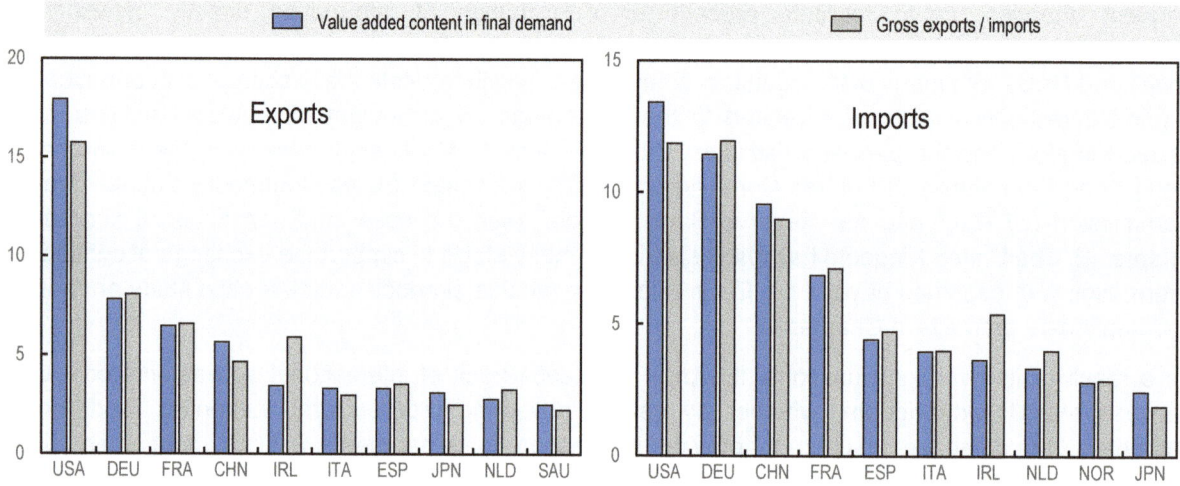

### Figure 3.2. Total UK trade

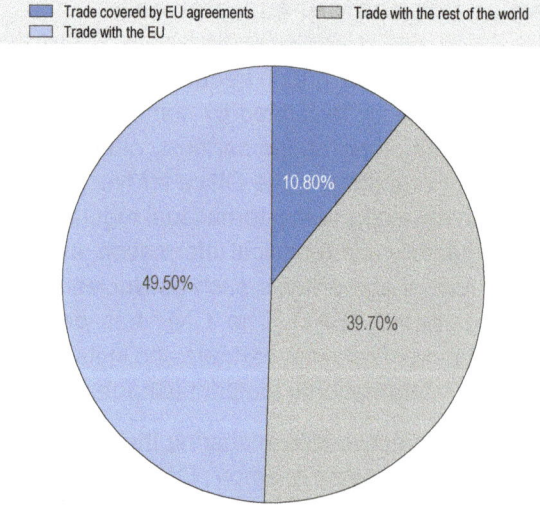

Note: Date period: year to end Q3 2018. The 10.8% excludes Turkey (plus San Marino and Andorra) which is part of a customs union with the EU, and excludes Japan, as the Economic Partnership Agreement only came into force on 1 February 2019.
Source: https://www.gov.uk/government/organisations/department-for-international-trade.

When it was an EU member state, the United Kingdom was a party to trade and mutual recognition agreements (MRAs) concluded by the EU. In that capacity, the UK participated in around 40 free trade agreements with over 70 countries,[8] accounting for some 10.8% of its trade, and recognised the authority of certain conformity assessment bodies from seven countries (Australia, Canada, Israel, Japan, New Zealand, Switzerland and the United States).[9]

The MRAs concluded by the EU, which covered the United Kingdom until the end of the transition period, differ in terms of sectoral coverage, structure and level of regulatory co-operation. To date, Switzerland and Canada have the most comprehensive mutual recognition agreements with the EU in terms of sectoral coverage (Annex B). All agreements include mechanisms for voluntary co-operation between regulators and procedures for investigations into CABs competence.

Among trade agreements concluded by the EU, the Comprehensive Economic and Trade Agreement (CETA) negotiated with Canada is the most advanced in terms of embedding systematic horizontal regulatory co-operation disciplines, with a long list of sectors covered and provisions for co-operation on a wide range of regulatory issues.[10] In particular, it establishes a Regulatory Co-operation Forum set up between Canada and the EU, which focuses on regulatory co-operation in five main areas: Cybersecurity and the Internet of Things; Animal Welfare, transportation of animals; Cosmetics-like drug products; Pharmaceutical inspections; Exchange of information between the EU RAPEX alert system and RADAR, Canada's consumer product incident reporting system.[11] CETA has been provisionally implemented in the United Kingdom since 21 September 2017, thus entailing that progress made in regulatory co-operation between Canada and the EU under CETA framework applied to the United Kingdom, until UK withdrawal from the EU.[12]

According to the EU – UK Withdrawal Agreement, all EU trade agreements continue to have effect during the transition period until 31st December 2020, and will cease to have legal effect in the United Kingdom at the end of this period.[13] The United Kingdom would then trade with all countries with whom it does not have a trade agreement under the terms agreed on in the WTO, and no longer under the more specific provisions of bilateral or regional trade agreements that often imply further integration. This means that all general provisions of WTO Agreements would apply, as well as tariff rates the United Kingdom has agreed on in the WTO context, with the principle of the "Most Favoured Nation".[14]

The United Kingdom is in the process of designing its own trade policy, which applies after the United Kingdom's exit from the EU. The Government introduced a Trade Bill in November 2017 to set the broad outlines of the upcoming UK Trade Policy. This bill aims to define how future trade agreements concluded by the United Kingdom will be developed and agreed on. It does not, however, establish a position on regulatory co-operation. However, this Bill did not complete its parliamentary process and will not become law.[15]

In addition, in order to ensure predictability in trade relations and prevent undue costs for businesses trading with the United Kingdom, the government has been working on "continuity agreements", which mostly replicate the provisions of trade agreements already agreed upon with the EU. The United Kingdom is seeking to provide continuity for existing EU free trade agreements covering around 70 countries that account for GBP 139bn or around 11% of UK total trade in 2018.[16] As of 4 June 2019, the United Kingdom had concluded agreements representing over half of the current total trade with countries where continuity for the existing EU trade agreements is sought. This includes some of UK's most important trading partners, such as Switzerland.[17] Although these agreements can be ratified, they will only take effect when existing EU trade agreements no longer apply to the UK, i.e. at the end of the transition period.[18] In the same way, to ensure continuity of benefits from MRAs, the United Kingdom has concluded continuity agreements with the following countries: Australia,[19] New Zealand,[20] and the US.[21] The United Kingdom has also concluded agreements with the US and Switzerland relating to insurance.[22]

Beyond these continuity agreements, the United Kingdom will also start negotiating new trade agreements with major trading partners. With this in mind, DIT has carried out a public consultation to prepare for negotiations with Australia, New Zealand, the US and the Comprehensive and Progressive Agreement for Trans-Pacific Partnership (CPTPP), and, more recently, Japan.[23] To accompany the consultation, the DIT has prepared an information note on trade with the specific countries, highlighting where trade barriers were highest, including non-tariff barriers (based on WTO's Integrated Trade Intelligence Portal for goods and the OECD Services Trade Restrictiveness Index for services) (see (Department for International Trade, 2018[2]); (Department for International Trade, 2018[3]); (Department for International Trade, 2018[4]). This type of information tailored to each trading partner would serve as a basis to direct the regulatory co-operation efforts to be embedded in each trade agreement. The consultation resulted in 600 000 responses, still being processed.

The UK government has also been working on trade and regulatory co-operation initiatives outside of the FTA sphere. For example in June 2018 the Chancellor for the Exchequer Rt Hon Philip Hammond MP announced a strategy to negotiate a series of Global Financial Partnerships (GFPs), which will "bring together governments, regulators, and industry to build an enhanced framework for cross-border financial services".[24]

## UK participation in regional *fora*

As EU member, the UK departments and regulators participated in a number of European regulatory agencies, bodies and networks – see the case studies in Chapter 4 for details on this participation for financial services, nuclear energy, product safety and medical and healthcare products. Back in 2017, the UK NAO reported some 34 European agencies whose frameworks affected the UK (National Audit Office, 2017[5]), plus a number of regulatory bodies and networks. These vehicles allowed UK departments and regulators to feed into their own domestic rulemaking (by co-operating actively with European peers, exchanging information and co-ordinating on enforcement activities), and to contribute to the development of regional positions, including in the preparation of EU Regulations and Directives. This dynamic process helped to ensure alignment of regulatory positions with regional peers. In addition, via European agencies' and bodies' ties with other regional networks or more global organisations, the United Kingdom also gained access to peers from non-EU countries.

The extent and modalities (if any) of UK participation in EU agencies and networks following the transition period remain unclear. There is also concern about whether "the extent of UK participation that is envisaged will be sufficient to ensure that UK interests are represented and fully taken into account" (House of Lords, 2019[6]). There is precedent for countries outside of the EU to participate in EU agencies – although participation in some such as the European Fisheries Control Agency and the Euratom Supply Agency is currently restricted to EU members. At present, membership status is usually reserved for EEA or EFTA member states, which can appoint experts to the relevant technical committees and working groups, as well as representatives on management boards (with limited or no voting rights on substantive matters). Participating as an observer country is also possible in the case of agencies that do not allow non-EU membership. Observer countries, which have no voting rights, can also participate in working groups and meetings. Compliance with relevant EU regulations and related provisions (e.g. monitoring and inspection) is usually a pre-requisite.

EEA/EFTA countries are currently members of the European Aviation Safety Agency, the European Food Safety Authority (EEA only) and the European Environment Agency. They have observer status in the European Chemical Agency, the European Medicines Agency, the Body of European Regulators for Electronic Communication (BEREC), the European Railway Agency, the European Banking Authority, the European Securities and Markets Authority and the European Insurance and Occupational Pensions Authority. Certain third countries also participate as observers in BEREC (Box 3.1), the European Aviation Safety Agency and the European Environment Agency. Although there is no precedent, participation as an observer in the European Chemical Agency and European Railway Agency would also be theoretically possible for third countries.

Co-operation between non-EU countries (without permanent member or observer status) and EU agencies can also be governed by administrative arrangements or MoUs. Agencies can invite those third countries to attend management board or committee meetings as observers (e.g. Europol can invite US authorities to management board meetings). The extent of co-operation under such agreements is however limited.

There is also opportunity to participate in other networks and initiatives that are not directly linked to EU membership. This is notably the case of RegWatchEurope, a network of external advisory bodies set up to "scrutinise the impacts of new legislation" and "challenge and advise […] governments on various aspects of better regulation and on the overall regulatory burden of legislation".[25] The UK's RPC is one of the network's members, as is the Better Regulation Council of Norway (a non-EU country).[26] Another example is the EU's NanoSafety Cluster[27] (NSC), one of whose Working Groups (WGG) focuses on the "use of scientific findings in different settings such as setting standards and developing internationally harmonised/accepted guidelines". The NSC, which is open to international partners, also encompasses the Malta Initiative, which serves "to develop and amend test guidelines and guidance documents to ensure that nano-specific issues for fulfilling regulatory requirements are addressed".[28]

---

**Box 3.1. Participation in EU bodies: the example of telecoms**

The UK Regulator for Communications Services (Ofcom) participates in a number of European regulatory agencies, bodies and networks, including the Body of European Regulators for Electronic Communications (BEREC).[1] BEREC is composed of national regulatory authorities from each EU member state responsible for overseeing the day-to-day operation of the markets for electronic communications networks and services.[2] Through this participation, OFCOM gains insights into how other national regulators are addressing policy challenges the United Kingdom is facing as well, and through a reciprocal exchange regulatory best practices are developed. As well as participating in working groups across BEREC's work programme, OFCOM can tap into other regulators' experiences by submitting questionnaires to BEREC members to know how they have addressed a particular regulatory issue.

In addition, through its participation in BEREC, OFCOM has had the opportunity to contribute to the development of EU-wide approaches to telecommunications regulation, thus helping to reduce regulatory divergences for private stakeholders operating throughout the EU. These common approaches are laid down in BEREC "guidelines" or "common positions", for example on information to be provided to consumers on mobile coverage,[3] on the implementation of EU rules on net neutrality, or on approaches to wholesale broadband access obligations.[4] As BEREC has an advisory role to the EU institutions in relation to European legislation, participation in BEREC has also enabled Ofcom to contribute to the development of the EU rules that have subsequently become binding in the United Kingdom.

Finally, BEREC has ties with regulatory authorities beyond the EU, and with other regional networks, allowing its members to increase ties with regulatory authorities from non-EU member states. For example, BEREC collaborates actively with its Latin American equivalent, Regulatel,[5] through yearly summits of the two groups. This allows all European regulators to cultivate ties with their peers in Latin America and share experiences and best practices on common challenges, such as promoting innovation, regulating for net neutrality or closing the digital divide and increasing the digitalisation of society.[6] BEREC also has memoranda of understanding with a number of regulators, including the FCC in the US, and TRAI in India.

> The extent and nature of OFCOM's continued participation in BEREC following the UK withdrawal from the EU will depend on the terms agreed on between the EU and UK by the end of the transition period. The recently adopted BEREC Regulation provides that BEREC is open to the participation of regulatory authorities from third countries to the EU "...with primary responsibility in the field of electronic communications, where those third countries have entered into agreements with the Union to that effect."[7]
>
> 1. https://berec.europa.eu/eng/about_berec/what_is_berec/.
> 2. https://berec.europa.eu/eng/about_berec/composition_and_organisation/.
> 3. https://berec.europa.eu/eng/document_register/subject_matter/berec/regulatory_best_practices/common_approaches_positions/8315-berec-common-position-on-information-to-consumers-on-mobile-coverage.
> 4. https://berec.europa.eu/eng/document_register/subject_matter/berec/regulatory_best_practices/common_approaches_positions/105-berecs-review-of-the-common-positions-on-wholesale-unbundled-access-wholesale-broadband-access-and-wholesale-leased-lines.
> 5. http://regulatel.org/w/.
> 6. https://berec.europa.eu/eng/document_register/subject_matter/berec/others/8297-berec-regulatel-summit-declaration.
> 7. Ibid.

## UK participation in multilateral *fora*

The United Kingdom has played an active role in contributing to a multilateral rule-based system through its active participation in international organisations. If anything, the broad context created by the United Kingdom's withdrawal from the EU, this has become an even stronger priority of UK foreign policy. Historically, the United Kingdom has played an important role in the development of international organisations, being a founding member of intergovernmental organisations such as NATO, OECD, WTO, the Council of Europe, OSCE, as well as more informal political *fora* such as the G7, G8 and the G20. It is also a permanent member of the United Nations Security Council.

Today, the UK departments and regulatory bodies participates actively in a variety of international organisations that develop normative instruments. These range from traditional intergovernmental organisations such as the Food and Agriculture Organisation (FAO), the International Atomic Energy Agency (IAEA), the World Health Organisation (WHO) or the OECD, to trans-governmental networks of regulators such as the International Organization of Securities Commissions (IOSCO) or the Pharmaceutical Inspection Co-operation Scheme (PIC/S).

To ensure active contribution to multilateral discussions, the United Kingdom has permanent delegations, responsible for covering the work of international organisations on a regular basis, at the OECD; the Commonwealth; the Council of Europe; the Organization for Security Co-operation in Europe (OSCE); NATO; the United Nations in Geneva and in New York; the International Monetary Fund (IMF); and the EU. These permanent delegations may cover the work of several international organisations in parallel. For example, the Geneva based mission to the United Nations covers the work of over 35 international organisations based in Switzerland, amounting to a UK contribution of approximately £2 billion a year.[29]

To support line ministries or sectoral regulators in the development of international legal instruments and standards in international organisations and where assistance is required, the FCO provides thematic and geographic advice to the relevant lead departments, both in London and by mobilising its network of permanent delegations. Beyond this, the FCO does not have a specific role in overseeing UK's participation in IOs, nor in ensuring that sectoral regulators and/or line ministries have a coherent position in IOs. A range of different departments hold the lead responsibility for engagement with the broad variety of international organisations which the UK participates in, depending on the subject matter covered.

Beyond intergovernmental organisations, BSI participates in international standardisation bodies such as ISO, IEC and ITU. BSI also participates with other UK bodies in ETSI.[30] By participating both in regional (European) and international fora, BSI plays a role in trying to ensure consistency between the standards developed at both levels. Via UKAS, the United Kingdom is also active in the International Accreditation Forum (IAF) and the International Laboratory Accreditation Cooperation (ILAC), the international associations promoting the value of accreditation against recognised national and international standards.

## References

Department for International Trade (2018), *An information pack for the consultation relating to a bilateral Free Trade Agreement between the United Kingdom and Australia*, https://assets.publishing.service.gov.uk/government/uploads/system/uploads/attachment_data/file/752616/Information_pack_UK_Australia_FTA_consultation.pdf. [3]

Department for International Trade (2018), *An information pack for the consultation relating to a bilateral Free Trade Agreement between the United Kingdom and New Zealand*, https://assets.publishing.service.gov.uk/government/uploads/system/uploads/attachment_data/file/752619/Information_pack_UK_New_Zealand_FTA_consultation.pdf. [2]

Department for International Trade (2018), *An information pack for the consultation relating to a bilateral Free Trade Agreement between the United Kingdom and the United States*, https://assets.publishing.service.gov.uk/government/uploads/system/uploads/attachment_data/file/752588/Information_pack_UK_US_FTA_consultation.pdf. [4]

Foreign and Commonwealth Office (2014), *Treaties and Memoranda of Understanding: Guidance on Practice and Procedures*, https://assets.publishing.service.gov.uk/government/uploads/system/uploads/attachment_data/file/293976/Treaties_and_MoU_Guidance.pdf (accessed on 27 February 2019). [1]

House of Lords (2019), "Beyond Brexit: how to win friends and influence people: 35th Report of Session 2017-19", *HL Paper 322*, https://publications.parliament.uk/pa/ld201719/ldselect/ldeucom/322/322.pdf. [6]

National Audit Office (2017), *A Short Guide to Regulation*, https://www.nao.org.uk/wp-content/uploads/2017/09/A-Short-Guide-to-Regulation.pdf. [5]

Regulatory Policy Committee (2018), *Comprehensive Economic and Trade Agreement (CETA) between the European Union and Canada Department for International Trade: RPC rating: fit for purpose*, https://assets.publishing.service.gov.uk/government/uploads/system/uploads/attachment_data/file/710646/RPC-4213_1_-DIT_CETA_Opinion.pdf. [7]

## Notes

[1] https://assets.publishing.service.gov.uk/government/uploads/system/uploads/attachment_data/file/840655/Agreement_on_the_withdrawal_of_the_United_Kingdom_of_Great_Britain_and_Northern_Ireland_from_the_European_Union_and_the_European_Atomic_Energy_Community.pdf.

[2] www.fca.org.uk/publication/mou/fca-circular-mrf-uk-hong-kong.pdf.

[3] https://publications.parliament.uk/pa/cm201011/cmselect/cmeuleg/633/63304.htm.

[4] www.fca.org.uk/publication/mou/supervisory-mou-fca-sfc.pdf.

[5] www.fca.org.uk/publication/mou/fca-cftc-mou-covered-firms.pdf.

[6] www.fca.org.uk/publication/mou/fsa-mou-rbi.pdf.

[7] https://treaties.fco.gov.uk/.

[8] http://ec.europa.eu/trade/policy/countries-and-regions/negotiations-and-agreements/#_in-place.

[9] https://ec.europa.eu/growth/single-market/goods/international-aspects/mutual-recognition-agreements_en.

[10] Although in relation to financial services, the UK benefits from the Regulatory Cooperation on Financial regulation Annex in the EU-Japan Economic Partnership Agreement. Key elements include a commitment to use recognition for each other's regimes wherever possible; considering the impact of new regulatory initiatives on the other Party; offering consultations on each other's rules, on a best endeavours basis; a process for withdrawal of any recognition granted; and the formation of a Joint Financial Regulatory Working Group.

[11] See UK RPC Opinion on impact assessment regarding CETA, (Regulatory Policy Committee, 2018[7]).

[12] www.gov.uk/government/collections/eu-canada-comprehensive-economic-and-trade-agreement-ceta.

[13] https://www.gov.uk/guidance/uk-trade-agreements-with-non-eu-countries.

[14] Ibid.

[15] https://services.parliament.uk/bills/2017-19/trade.html.

[16] This excludes Turkey (plus San Marino and Andorra) which is part of a customs union with the EU, and excludes Japan, as the Economic Partnership Agreement only came into force on 1 February 2019.

[17] https://www.gov.uk/guidance/uk-trade-agreements-with-non-eu-countries.

[18] https://www.gov.uk/guidance/uk-trade-agreements-with-non-eu-countries#trade-agreements-that-have-been-signed.

[19] www.gov.uk/government/news/uk-and-australia-agree-continuity-of-mutual-recognition-agreement.

[20] www.gov.uk/government/publications/cs-new-zealand-no22019-uknew-zealand-agreement-on-mutual-recognition-in-relation-to-conformity-assessment.

[21] www.gov.uk/guidance/signed-uk-trade-agreements-transitioned-from-the-eu.

[22] https://www.gov.uk/government/news/switzerland-and-uk-to-sign-post-brexit-insurance-deal.

[23] www.gov.uk/government/publications?departments%5B%5D=department-for-international-trade&publication_filter_option=consultations.

[24] www.gov.uk/government/speeches/mansion-house-2018-speech-by-the-chancellor-of-the-exchequer and www.gov.uk/government/speeches/china-and-the-uk-committed-partners-to-open-trade-and-free-markets.

[25] www.regwatcheurope.eu/.

[26] It is worth noting that RegWatchEurope is looking to expand to new non-EU members such as Iceland.

[27] www.nanosafetycluster.eu/.

[28] www.nanosafetycluster.eu/international-cooperation/the-malta-initiative/.

[29] www.gov.uk/world/organisations/uk-mission-to-the-united-nations-geneva.

[30] ETSI is open to membership buy large and small private companies, research entities, academia, government and public organisations. One hundred and eleven bodies from the UK are members of ETSI.

# 4 Sectoral case studies

This chapter provides case studies describing the international regulatory co-operation practices in four sectors: financial services, nuclear energy, medical and healthcare products and product safety. These sectors represent areas in which there is strong rationale for international regulatory co-operation because of the transboundary policy challenges that are raised, and where the United Kingdom has been particularly active in IRC efforts, either at the bilateral, regional or multilateral levels.

# Financial services

HM Treasury has acknowledged the vital importance of IRC for "the ability of UK financial services to compete in international markets" and the country's economic attractiveness in its *Financial Services Future Regulatory Framework Review*.

Major areas of financial regulation are set at EU level.[1] This is the case for prudential regulation of banks, investment firms and insurers, the regulation of financial markets, and conduct regulation of key financial products such as insurance and retail investment products, as well as sectors such as payment services and consumer credit.

Beyond these traditional areas of financial regulation (and to support them), the United Kingdom has developed a number of bilateral co-operation initiatives on financial issues. The country also aims to work multilaterally where issues are cross-border or common to many jurisdictions. As an example, and building upon the Financial Conduct Authority (FCA)'s 2018 proposal to create a "global" regulatory sandbox, the United Kingdom contributed to the launch of the Global Financial Innovation Network (GFIN) in January 2019, an international group of financial regulators and related organisations. The GFIN represents an attempt to apply at the multilateral level the FinTech bridges' bilateral co-operation agreement model pioneered by the United Kingdom.

The United Kingdom is also increasingly focusing on multilateral initiatives relating to money laundering, terrorist financing and other related threats to the integrity of the international financial system. A promising initiative that is currently being explored in this regard is the enhanced multilateral co-operation between law enforcement entities and banks (as well as within each of those groups of actors).

## *Main rationale for international regulatory co-operation in the sector*

The financial services sector is of major importance for the UK's economy. In 2018, it accounted for nearly 7% of the country's GDP and about 3% of all jobs (Rhodes, 2019[1]). Moreover, the United Kingdom is a leading exporter of financial services across the world. This sector of activity accounted for 23% of all UK service exports and 9% of all service imports in 2017, and has consistently yielded trade surpluses over the years (Rhodes, 2019[1]). In addition, London is an international financial hub attracting substantial amounts of FinTech investment (more than USD 16bn in the first half of 2018, or about 28% of the world's total) (TheCityUK, 2018[2]).

Strong IRC is therefore essential if the United Kingdom is to retain its leadership and continue to promote innovative regulatory approaches. IRC is also crucial to ensure business continuity in the context of Brexit. The EU is the UK's largest financial services export market (43% of exports and 34% of imports in 2017), and UK banks have subsidiaries in many EU member states. Moreover, the development of the EU's single market for financial services resulted in the expansion of EU legislation applying to financial services, and post-crisis reforms led to "a certain degree of centralisation and transfer of responsibility from the national to EU level in many aspects of financial services regulation and supervision".[2] Key areas of regulation, which are set at the EU level, include the prudential regulation of banks, investment firms and insurers, the regulation of financial markets, and conduct regulation of key financial products such as insurance and retail investment products (HM Treasury, 2019[3]).

HM Treasury recently acknowledged the importance of IRC in its "Financial Services Future Regulatory Framework Review". According to the Review, "… an optimally designed regulatory framework should facilitate co-operation and the development of common standards across international regulatory bodies and jurisdictions, and support the ability of UK financial services to compete in international markets, as well as ensuring that the United Kingdom is open and attractive to new and existing trading partners" (HM Treasury, 2019[3]).

## UK bodies involved

At the domestic level, responsibility for financial regulation in the United Kingdom is shared between the following bodies:[3]

- HM Treasury: focuses on the overall institutional structure of financial regulation (including negotiation of European legislation when the UK was a member of the EU).
- Bank of England (BoE, including the Financial Policy Committee, or FPC): responsible for macroprudential regulation and overall resilience of the financial sector.
- Prudential Regulation Authority (PRA): the UK's prudential regulator for deposit takers, insurers and designated investment firms.
- Financial Conduct Authority (FCA): the conduct supervisor of all UK regulated firms, prudential supervisor for those firms not falling under PRA's prudential supervision, including asset managers, mortgage and insurance brokers. The FCA is also responsible for the regulation of UK's primary and secondary markets. It works closely with HMT, the BoE, the PRA and the FPC.
- Payment Systems Regulator (PSR): a subsidiary of the FCA that regulates the payment systems industry (including through standard setting and actions to safeguard competition).

UK representation in international fora on financial regulation is spread across several authorities including HM Treasury, the BoE, the FCA and the PRA. There is also involvement from the Foreign and Commonwealth Office (FCO) and the Department for International Trade (DIT) (chiefly on economic and financial dialogues and discussions about financial services in trade agreements). An MoU exists for consultation and co-operation amongst the authorities representing the country in the different fora.[4] It allocates international representation roles to the various UK institutions, acknowledging that the list of interested parties is not comprehensive and that, in some international organisations, there is "scope for flexibility in sub-committee or working group participation". This MoU aims at ensuring consistency in the UK's position and line in discussions with international partners. It establishes an International Coordination Committee that is responsible for ensuring that the UK authorities act in accordance with its principles. The MoU, which is an example of good practice (as it ensures transparency and considers implementation aspects) is to be reviewed "at least annually".

## Bilateral co-operation initiatives

Bilateral co-operation activities between the United Kingdom and other countries on financial regulation take a variety of forms, which differ in terms of depth and scope. Previous agreements with major economic partners have taken the form of joint statements. Most of them focus primarily on information exchange but the most recent ones have targeted the compatibility of the countries' respective rules. Co-operation may also take the form of dialogue fora or technical assistance projects (typically with smaller partners).

Regulatory co-operation with major economic partners tends to unfold within the framework of larger co-operation initiatives that go beyond regulatory matters (e.g. macroeconomic policies, infrastructure development, trade agreements etc.). For example, the Economic and Financial Dialogues (EFDs) with China,[5] India[6] and Brazil,[7] take place on an annual or biennial basis and are led by the Chancellor of the Exchequer (the FCA and the Bank of England are also involved), and aim to strengthen communication and increase co-operation between the United Kingdom and these markets.

The U.S.-UK Financial Regulatory Working Group was created in April 2018 to formalise the two countries' bilateral regulatory co-operation engagement, notably in the context of "the transition in the UK's regulatory relationship with the EU due to Brexit".[8] A joint statement announced its creation in April 2018 as a forum "to exchange views on the regulatory relationship between the United States and the UK". It gathers officials and senior staff from the U.S. Department of the Treasury and HM Treasury, and from the U.S. and UK independent regulatory agencies. The statement suggests a higher level of ambition compared to co-operation with the abovementioned emerging economies in that it aims to "improve transparency, reduce uncertainty, identify potential cross-border implementation issues, work towards avoiding regulatory arbitrage and towards compatibility, as appropriate, of each other's national laws and regulations".[9] The joint statement that followed the Working Group's second meeting in May 2019 highlighted discussions about "financial regulatory reforms and future priorities, including possible areas for deeper regulatory co-operation to facilitate further safe and efficient financial services activity".

In addition, the UK has entered a series of broader dialogue fora with countries including Japan, Korea, Singapore, Hong-Kong and Switzerland. These may be formalised through an MoU (but not necessarily) and keep a flexible agenda in order to focus on areas of mutual interest. They usually focus strongly on information exchange.

FCA has concluded MoUs with many of its regulatory counterparts to facilitate the exchange of information and support investigative assistance related to the supervision and oversight of regulated entities in the United Kingdom and the partner jurisdiction. Examples include MoUs signed between the FCA and the Hong Kong Securities and Futures Commission (SFC),[10] the United States Commodity Futures Trading Commission (CFTC),[11] and the Reserve Bank of India.[12]

Given the growing importance of regulatory issues relating to the FinTech sector, since 2016 the United Kingdom has set up a number of "FinTech bridges", which are bilateral co-operation agreements "outlining collaboration between two governments, co-operation between regulatory bodies and connectivity between two markets and ecosystems". Fintech bridges are co-developed by DIT, HMT and FCA and serve to facilitate compliance and enhance market access for FinTech companies and promote trade and investment with priority international markets for UK firms. Each bridge is underpinned by a co-operation agreement signed by the FCA. Some enable a referral mechanism for already licensed firms that meet specific criteria seeking authorisation in corresponding markets; others enable a referral mechanism for already licensed firms that meet specific criteria seeking authorisation in corresponding markets. Countries with which the United Kingdom has concluded this kind of agreements are listed in Table 4.1.[13]

### Table 4.1. UK Fintech bridge agreements

| Country | Institution |
| --- | --- |
| Australia | Australian Securities and Investments Commission |
| China | People's Bank of China |
| Hong Kong | Hong Kong's Securities and Future Commissions (SFC) |
| Korea | Korean Financial Services Commission |
| Singapore | Monetary Authority of Singapore |

Source: Information provided by HMT and FCA.

### Engagement in regional or international bodies / initiatives

With increasingly global and interdependent financial markets, rules to govern them are increasingly being set at the regional and multilateral level. The bulk of EU legislation in this area has been transposed into domestic UK law. In the same vein, the country has adopted all main international instruments.

Whilst the United Kingdom was still a member of the EU, the UK Treasury and FCO represented the United Kingdom at the Council of the European Union's meetings on financial services legislation. Treasury also engaged with the European Commission, which is responsible for initiating new legislative proposals. The UK regulators engaged with European supervisory authorities, such as the European Securities and Markets Authority (ESMA), the European Banking Authority (which has recently relocated from London to

Paris ahead of the withdrawal from the EU) and the European Insurance and Occupational Pensions Authority, and were able to vote on proposed Binding Technical Standards.[14]

The United Kingdom has played an active role over the years in the activities of the Financial Stability Board (FSB), an international body that promotes the reform of international financial regulation and supervision[15] and is responsible for monitoring implementation of relevant standards (e.g. for solvency and liquidity). Bank of England Governor Mark Carney served as Chair of the FSB between 2011 and 2018. Representatives from Treasury, FCA and the Bank of England attend FSB's plenary meetings and are members of its standing committees. There is regular co-operation across the different UK bodies involved in the different committees to ensure consistency.

The FCA and Bank of England also engage extensively with the international organisations, including the Basel Committee on Banking Supervision, the International Organization of Securities Commissions (IOSCO), and the International Association of Insurance Supervisors. The United Kingdom (via the FCA) is among the signatories of IOSCO's Multilateral Memorandum of Understanding (MMoU) Concerning Consultation and Cooperation and the Exchange of Information,[16] which emerged as a response from regulators to the increasing international activity in the securities and derivatives markets [17] and provides a useful framework exchanging confidential information for the purpose of regulatory enforcement, thus facilitating cross-border co-operation. The FCA has been actively involved in developing and enhancing the MMoU over time, and regularly uses the MMoU as the basis for co-operating with its international counterparts. It has also been actively involved in IOSCO's enforcement and co-operation committee as well as in the development of the new, enhanced MMoU (the FCA having been its first EU signatory).

Moreover, the FCA works extensively with the Financial Action Task Force (FATF), an inter-governmental body promoting national legislative and regulatory reforms pertaining to money laundering, terrorist financing and other related threats to the integrity of the international financial system.[18] According to FCA officials, their efforts in this context focus increasingly on multilateral initiatives. A promising initiative that is currently being explored in this regard has to do with enhanced co-operation between law enforcement entities and banks (as well as within each of those groups of actors) on money laundering and terrorist financing. Successful co-operation examples of this kind already exist in certain national jurisdictions such as Australia and Hong Kong. Table 4.2 outlines the UK authorities represented in selected relevant international organisations, as per the MoU.

The United Kingdom is also active launching new multilateral initiatives. The Global Financial Innovation Network (GFIN) was launched in January 2019 by an international group of financial regulators and related organisations, including the FCA.[19] It builds on the FCA's 2018 proposal to create a "global" regulatory sandbox.[20] Its main functions are:

- To act as a network of regulators to collaborate and share experience of innovation in respective markets, including emerging technologies and business models, and to provide accessible regulatory contact information for firms.
- To provide a forum for joint RegTech work and collaborative knowledge sharing/lessons learned.
- To provide firms with an environment in which to trial cross-border solutions.

Regulators involved launched a pilot phase of cross-border testing (for firms) in January 2019, receiving over 40 applications from firms based around the world. The pilot, which is still ongoing at the time of writing, will inform the future direction GFIN takes with regards to future cross-border testing activity.

## Table 4.2. UK authorities represented in selected international organisations dealing with financial regulation

| Organisation | UK representative(s) (voting) | Other interested parties may include |
|---|---|---|
| EU Council, including EU Financial Services Committee | HMT | PRA, FCA |
| European Banking Authority (EBA) | PRA | FCA, BoE |
| European Securities and Markets Authority (ESMA) | FCA | BoE, FRC |
| European Insurance and Occupational Pensions Authority (EIOPA) | PRA | TPR, FCA |
| European Systemic Risk Board (ESRB) | BoE | PRA, FCA |
| Financial Stability Board (FSB) | HMT, BoE, FCA | PRA |
| Basel Committee on Banking Supervision (BCBS) | PRA | BoE, FCA |
| Bank of International Settlements (BIS) | BoE | |
| International Organisation of Securities Commissions (IOSCO) | FCA | BoE |
| International Association of Insurance Supervisors (IAIS) | FCA, PRA | |
| OECD | HMT | BoE, FCO, FCA |

Note: the Bank of England (BoE), the Financial Conduct Authority (FCA), the Foreign and Commonwealth Office (FCO), the Prudential Regulatory Authority (PRA), the Pensions Regulator (TPR), and Treasury (HMT).
Source: Bank of England.

### *Outstanding challenges*

Among the four long-term challenges identified by the Chancellor of the Exchequer with regard to the UK's financial services sector, two refer explicitly to IRC. The first one has to do with operating outside the EU. Key areas of UK financial regulation are currently set at EU level. Regulatory arrangements will therefore need to be adapted "to reflect the UK's new position outside of the EU and its single market for financial services". The second challenge lies with the opening of the UK's regulatory framework to new markets beyond Europe, and "support the development of new trading relationships as well as facilitating co-operation on international standards and supervision".[21]

In terms of thematic areas, IRC's relevance is particularly noteworthy in the context of a rapid development of cryptocurrency exchange services and virtual assets and its implications for the application of legislation on anti-money laundering/combating the financing of terrorism. IRC can be instrumental in helping develop regulatory approaches that effectively address related challenges (often involving transnational actors).[22] International peer review mechanisms in this area have also been highlighted as potential means for sharing best practices and building the necessary capacity at regulatory and enforcement bodies. The UK Parliament reflected upon the role of IRC in this area as part of its 2018 "Crypto-assets" report by noting that "given the UK has yet to introduce any crypto-asset regulation, it is in a position to learn from those experience of countries that have done so".[23] In their joint response to the inquiry report, the UK government and FCA envisage that "the UK will be a thought leader in shaping future regulatory approaches".[24]

## Nuclear energy

The regulatory environment governing civil nuclear activities is global in nature. This is due to the sector's high level of internationalisation as well as to the need for worldwide regulatory co-operation to preserve nuclear safety and security by upholding the highest standards. The United Kingdom has been active internationally to promote IRC as a means of influencing the development of international standards, guidance and relevant good practice so they help achieve domestic regulatory objectives and support high levels of safety and security worldwide.

As a result of the sector's international scope, IRC in this area cuts across the EU's borders to involve nuclear powers such as the US, Japan, China and India. The Office for Nuclear Regulation (ONR) is both strongly connected internationally and deeply aware of IRC's relevance, as illustrated by the publication of the *Strategic Framework for International Engagement to 2025* in May 2019. This innovative framework notably develops the notion of *International Footprint*, which articulates the full set of potential benefits from IRC, defines strategic priorities to reap those benefits and sets out a long-term vision for the UK's international engagement in this area. This approach is expected to help UK authorities monitor and ensure fulfilment of the country's international commitments and gain a deeper understanding of the impact of their IRC activities in terms of contribution to their own strategic agenda as well as influence beyond domestic borders.

From 1973 to the EU withdrawal, the UK was part of the Treaty establishing the European Atomic Energy Community (Euratom), which encompasses a safeguards regime applying to all nuclear facilities and movements of nuclear products and materials in the United Kingdom. Euratom safeguards enabled the United Kingdom to abide by its non-proliferation requirements under international law. As part of the Withdrawal Agreement, the United Kingdom has accepted its sole responsibility for the continued performance of nuclear safeguards and its commitment to a future regime that provides coverage and effectiveness equivalent to existing Euratom arrangements.[25] Beyond this, a safeguards regime will need to be put in place by the time the country leaves the EU and Euratom at the end of 2020 if damaging disruptions to supply and trade in nuclear materials are to be avoided. The UK Government has proposed a wide ranging civil nuclear co-operation agreement with Euratom that is expected to encompass a co-operation mechanism between ONR, as the UK's Safeguards regulator, the State System of Accountancy and Control of Nuclear Materials (SSAC), and Euratom (ONR, 2019[4]).

The UK regulators' strong international connections mean that the country is in a good position to promote further efforts to ensure a consistent approach to regulating emerging technological innovation in the field of nuclear energy. This could build upon existing information and best practice exchanges with partner countries (including at the SMR Regulators' Forum) but may also warrant innovative co-operation modalities that help develop a suitable regulatory environment.

### Main rationale for international regulatory co-operation in the sector

As stated in the *Strategic Framework for International Engagement to 2025* published by the ONR in May 2019 (Box 4.1), hereinafter "the Framework" (ONR, 2019[5]),[26] "the global nature of the nuclear industry and the potential trans-boundary impact of any severe nuclear accident" mean that the United Kingdom will need to step up its engagement in IRC in the years to come. In the same vein, the Framework refers to IRC as a means to "influence standard-setting globally and ensure their output takes account of UK regulatory practice and meets the UK needs". Historically, the United Kingdom has been co-operating significantly on nuclear safety issues in the EU and beyond the EU, both bilaterally and multilaterally.

The UK withdrawal from Euratom has implications, in the absence of a formal agreement with Euratom, for the security of supply of nuclear materials and the ability to promote nuclear medicine research. IRC appears to be essential in order to avoid disruptions in this respect.

---

#### Box 4.1. ONR's Framework for International Engagement

The Framework is a rare example of strategic thinking around IRC in a specific sector. It aims to:

- Define priority objectives and criteria (e.g. to assess the potential merits of participating in international fora and events other than those identified as priority engagement) for international engagement over the period to 2025, and

> - Systematically assess the effectiveness of IRC based on evidence.
>
> To do so, it relies on the notion of International Footprint, which articulates the full set of potential benefits from IRC, defines strategic priorities to reap those benefits and sets out a long-term vision for the UK's international engagement in this area. In this context, objective 1 on the Framework's first strategic theme is "To influence the development of international standards, guidance and relevant good practice to ensure they are fit of purpose to achieve UK regulatory objectives and support high levels of safety and security across the globe through our own learning and sharing our expertise". This approach is expected to help UK authorities monitor and ensure fulfilment of the country's international commitments and gain a deeper understanding of the impact of their IRC activities in terms of its contribution to their own strategic agenda as well as influence beyond domestic borders.
>
> The Framework is to be reviewed on an annual basis in order to reflect shifting priorities as well as international and political developments. An internal International Steering Group (ISG) will provide corporate oversight to ensure alignment across ONR's international activities. The key objectives of the ISG are to:
>
> - "Ensure ONR's international engagement is well-planned, prioritised and aligned to the Framework; use this information to monitor to what extent the strategy objectives are met and provide advice on where objectives may need to change"
> - "Act in an advisory capacity on international business priorities informed by an analysis of ONR's 'international travel pattern'
> - "Ensure international engagements are appropriately authorised, clearly linked to worthwhile strategic objective(s), and with justifiable benefits; and provide appropriate challenge where this is no clear alignment"
> - "Baseline international activities and their impact through robust evidence-based data".

## UK bodies involved

Key UK public bodies involved in nuclear energy-related IRC are the ONR and the FCO, which co-ordinate closely with each other. The former typically participates in committee meetings of relevant standard-setting organisations, whereas the latter operates through the country's permanent missions. The Secretary of State for the Department for Business, Energy and Industrial Strategy (BEIS), in turn, has overall responsibility for the UK's civil nuclear regulatory framework and policies, including preparations for the UK's withdrawal from the EU.[27] In this sense, it is worth noting that in its Framework ONR foresees to "develop and agree a streamlined framework and formal process with the Department of Business, Energy and Industrial Strategy (BEIS)". Other bodies involved in multilateral standard-setting processes are the Department for Transport (DfT) and the National Information Infrastructure (NII).[28]

## Bilateral co-operation initiatives

UK authorities co-operate with a range of regulatory bodies in EU as well as non-EU countries. These include mature nuclear powers as well as aspirant nuclear nations. According to the Framework, the ONR is "committed to working with aspirant nuclear nations to support the development of high standards of safety and security" and sees itself as having a role to play "in raising the bar internationally for public protection" and "supporting Government's interactions with like-minded pro-nuclear countries and those where the UK seeks to influence non-proliferation efforts".

Formal agreements typically take the form of either Nuclear Cooperation Agreements (NCAs) or Information Exchange Arrangements (IEAs) (Table 4.3).

NCAs are legally binding, bilateral agreements negotiated between two States (or international bodies) covering co-operation in the civil nuclear sector. According to BEIS, "every NCA is different and is negotiated on a case-by-case basis". While they allow states to formally recognise their willingness to co-operate with each other, they do not normally commit either side to undertake any specific activity (BEIS, 2018[6]).

IEAs, in turn, are bilateral agreements with other nuclear regulators to "share information, experience and good practice where it is believed to be mutually beneficial and in the UK's national interests". ONR points out that "it does not have IEAs with every country with which it exchanges information, as mutual co-operation is often achieved informally between signatories of the various international conventions". Like NCAs, each IEA differs, although they frequently cover information concerning the regulation of siting, construction, commissioning, operation, transport of radioactive material, radioactive waste management and decommissioning of civil nuclear installations, preparedness and management of nuclear and radiological emergencies.[29] Consulted ONR officials highlighted the existence of regular exchanges of information on inspections, enforcement and "nuclear innovation" with partner countries. In this respect, they singled out co-operation with Japanese authorities to improve inspection practices. Information exchanges were also identified as a valuable source of evidence in the context of the upcoming post implementation review of the Energy Act, which is to take place in 2021.

Table 4.3. UK bilateral regulatory co-operation in the nuclear energy sector

| Current Nuclear Co-operation Agreements | Current Information Exchange Arrangements | Countries to which ONR has provided experts for IRRS missions (2014-16) | Countries to which ONR has provided experts for IPPAS missions (2014-present) |
| --- | --- | --- | --- |
| China, India, Jordan, Japan (complementing the Euratom-Japan NCA), Korea, Russian Federation, United Arab Emirates. | Canada, China, Finland, France, Ireland, India, Japan, Poland, South Africa, Sweden, United Arab Emirates, United States of America | Belgium, China, Hungary, India, Japan, Korea, Lithuania, Kazakhstan, Netherlands, Poland, Romania, Slovakia, South Africa, Spain, Sweden | Austria, Belgium, Canada, China, France, Japan, Lithuania, Romania, Sweden, Switzerland, United Arab Emirates |

Source: ONR.

In addition to NCAs and IEAs, bilateral regulatory co-operation also takes place as part of international co-operation initiatives. In the context of the International Atomic Energy Agency's Integrated Regulatory Review Service (IRRS), the ONR provides experts for review missions in other countries. In the same vein, the United Kingdom hosts and contributes experts to missions by the International Physical Protection Advisory Service (IPPAS), which cover nuclear security practices.

### Engagement in regional or international bodies / initiatives

ONR co-operates extensively with international organisations to "influence globally, learn from relevant international good practice and maintain alignment with international obligations, standards and conventions". IRC allows the United Kingdom to keep abreast with regulatory developments and ensure that multilateral approaches under development take into account the country's needs and specificities. Worldwide regulatory co-operation is indeed all the more important given the potential consequences of a nuclear accident and the associated need to uphold the highest safety and security standards. To this end, UK authorities notably participate in the work of the International Atomic Energy Agency (IAEA), the European Nuclear Security Regulators Association, the Western European Nuclear Regulators Association (WENRA), the Nuclear Energy Agency (NEA), the World Institute for Nuclear Security and the International Regulators Conference on Nuclear Security (Box 4.2).

The United Kingdom became part of Euratom in 1973, when it joined the European Economic Community. Euratom encompasses a safeguards regime applying to all nuclear facilities and movements of nuclear products and materials in the United Kingdom. According to a spokesperson for the UK Nuclear Industry Association (NIA), Euratom safeguards preventing nuclear material from being diverted from civil nuclear power for other means and thus enable the United Kingdom to abide by its non-proliferation requirements under international law. As a member of Euratom, the United Kingdom had co-operation agreements with eight other countries, including Australia, Kazakhstan and Canada, which between them account for more than 70% of uranium production worldwide (NS Energy, 2018[7]). Euratom also regulates the supply of the isotopes used in nuclear medicine.

To avoid damaging disruptions in any of these areas arising from the UK's withdrawal from the EU and Euratom, the UK Government has proposed a new civil nuclear relationship based on a wide ranging NCA with Euratom (ONR, 2019[4]). This NCA is expected to include a co-operation mechanism between ONR, as the UK's Safeguards regulator and State System of Accountancy and Control of Nuclear Materials (SSAC), and Euratom. ONR is also a member of the European Safeguards Research and Development Association (ESARDA) and, intends, according to the Framework, to remain so and "enhance its role in ESARDA's work as the UK leaves Euratom" (ONR, 2019[4]).

---

**Box 4.2. Selected examples of UK multilateral regulatory co-operation in the nuclear energy sector**

**International Atomic Energy Agency (IAEA)**

ONR participates in the IAEA's Commission on Safety Standards (CSS) and the Safety Standards Committees (NUSSC, WASSC, RASSC, TRANSSC, and EPRSC). IAEA safety standards, which are not binding on states, encompass principles, requirements and guidance, and are applicable throughout the entire lifetime of facilities and activities. On its website, ONR indicates that, in the United Kingdom, these standards were notably used to benchmark a recent review of Safety Assessment Principles for Nuclear Facilities and in the review of the Technical Assessment Guides.

ONR also takes part in meetings of the Nuclear Security Guidance Committee (NSGC) and its Standing Advisory Group on Safeguards Implementation (SAGSI), and inputs to IAEA's annual General Conference (including the Senior Regulators Conference).

**OECD Nuclear Energy Agency (NEA)**

ONR staff attend a number of working groups and task groups, the output of which "provides demonstrable and proven value" in the context of developing regulatory technical assessment and inspection guides. According to the Framework, the UK Government, in liaison with ONR, "is seeking to maximise engagement with NEA and increase co-ordination to better influence best practice in line with UK objectives".

**Multinational Design Evaluation Programme (MDEP)**

ONR is a member of MDEP, which encompasses national regulatory authorities from 16 countries (which retain their sovereign authority to make licensing and regulatory decisions) and focuses on facilitating more efficient and effective assessments of new reactor power plant designs. MDEP plays an important role in developing approaches to regulating the supply chain (quality of nuclear safety-related components). According to the Framework, ONR will, "in part through the MDEP supply chain working group, continue international co-operation in […] regulation of the supply chain to gain assurance of the quality of nuclear safety-related components".[1] ONR's Chief Nuclear Inspector chairs the MDEP Policy Group. ONR also chairs the EPR design-specific working group, which focuses "on developing standards and sharing experience in the regulation of commissioning for EPRs under construction".

**Small Modular Reactors Regulators' Forum**

ONR participates in the Small Modular Reactor (SMR) Regulators' Forum, which operates under the auspices of the IAEA. According to ONR's website, this forum has helped the UK to identify relevant high-level regulatory challenges pertaining to SMRs as well as to meet the objectives of ONR's Advanced Nuclear Technologies project.

1 ONR Strategic Framework for International Engagement to 2025, p. 5 ff. In the same section, the Framework also mentions ONR's involvement in the work of the European Nuclear Security Regulators Association (ENSRA) ("Historically, there has been inadequate alignment between WENRA and ENSRA and it has been recognised there is a need for a more integrated approach", p. 7) as well as of the World Institute for Nuclear Security (WINS) ("The UK contributes to its funding and the ONR is prominent in the support of and input to its document development", p. 8).
Source: Summary from (ONR, 2019[5]).

### *Outstanding challenges*

Looking ahead, a number of challenges deserve particular attention. These are acknowledged in the Framework.

- To avoid any disruptions to the UK's civil nuclear activities, it will be important to remain committed to nuclear safety and security across Europe by implementing relevant provisions under Euratom Directives transposed into UK law and pursuing its international engagement to ensure the existence of a suitable post-Brexit safeguards regimes.
- Efforts will need to be deployed to ensure a consistent approach to regulating emerging technological innovation in the field of nuclear energy. This could build upon existing information and best practice exchanges with partner countries (including at the SMR Regulators' Forum) but may also warrant innovative co-operation modalities that help develop a suitable regulatory environment.

## Medical and healthcare products

Whilst the UK was a member of the EU, the UK's pharmaceutical and medical products sector operated within a Europe-wide "unique regulatory framework", with the European Medicines Agency (EMA) at its core. This system allowed greater certainty thanks to consistent standards across the continent, administrative burden minimisations through a centralised authorisation procedure, and improved information exchange and market surveillance.

These benefits could be at risk depending on the withdrawal arrangements agreed on between the EU and the UK. In addition, although UK regulators are actively engaged in regulatory co-operation beyond the European continent leaving that system may jeopardise the country's ability to influence regulatory discussions at international fora such as the International Council on Harmonisation of Technical Requirements for Registration of Pharmaceuticals for Human Use (ICH), where the UK participated as part of the EU delegation.

The UK government has stated its willingness to pursue a close relationship with EMA as well as the EU regulatory network on medicines and medical device regulation. The country put in place contingency legislation allowing the continued sale of and access to medicines to mitigate for a non-deal exit from the EU. In recent years, it has also intensified its bilateral regulatory engagement, including with key actors such as China, the United States and Canada.

While continued full membership of EMA does not seem to be an option after withdrawal from the EU (no provisions exist for third countries to become members or observers at the EMA), EMA maintains a network of agreements with non EU countries such as Switzerland, the United States and Canada that provide models for consideration.

### Main rationale for international regulatory co-operation in the sector

According to a representative of the Medicines and Healthcare Products Regulatory Agency (MHRA), "working in an increasingly global environment, the sharing of intelligence between medicines regulators is the cornerstone of protecting the health system worldwide".[30] In addition, strong regulatory co-operation is particularly important for frictionless cross-border trade in pharmaceuticals, as supply chains for medicines are deeply integrated and often involve production processes that span a number of countries.

Generally speaking, the United Kingdom is heavily dependent on the EU market for medicines and healthcare products. UK exports of pharmaceutical products were worth an estimated GBP 23.5 billion (about EUR 21.2 billion) in 2018, 46% of which to EU countries; whereas UK imports of pharmaceutical products were worth GBP 23.4 billion in 2017, 76% of which from EU countries.[31]

The European medicines regulatory system is based on a network of around 50 regulatory authorities from the 31 EEA countries, the European Commission and the European Medicines Agency (EMA). EMA works with national bodies, including from the United Kingdom, in the regulation and licensing of medicines and medical devices and monitoring of their safety. Based on the single EU regulatory system for pharmaceuticals, confidential information is exchanged between the EU member states and results of inspections carried out by any of the EU member states are automatically recognised by all. According to EMA, this regulatory system offers the following benefits:[32]

- Enables member states to pool resources and co-ordinate work to regulate medicines efficiently and effective
- Creates certainty for patients, healthcare professionals, industry and governments by ensuring consistent standards and use of best available expertise
- Reduces the administrative burden through the centralised authorisation procedure, helping medicines to reach patients faster
- Accelerates the exchange of information on important issues, such as the safety of medicines.

### UK bodies involved

As explained in a UK Parliament research briefing (House of Commons, 2019[8]):

> "There are currently two regulatory bodies through which UK medicines can be licensed, medical devices are regulated, and a medicine's safety is monitored. The European Medicines Agency performs all these roles on an EU and EEA (European Economic Area) countrywide basis. The Medicines and Healthcare Products Regulatory Agency (MHRA) is the UK-based regulator. The MHRA sits within the Department of Health and Social Care. Among the responsibilities listed on its website is "influencing UK, EU and international regulatory frameworks so that they're risk-proportionate and effective at protecting public health".

### Bilateral co-operation initiatives

The EU regulatory system for medicines allows EU member states to sign individual bilateral arrangements[33] with third countries. In recent years, the United Kingdom has intensified its bilateral regulatory engagement beyond the EU, including with key actors such as China, the US and Canada.

In February 2019, the United Kingdom and the United States signed a MRA on Conformity Assessment, including for pharmaceuticals, that will maintain all relevant aspects of the current EU-US MRA once it ceases to apply to the United Kingdom (so "UK exporters can continue to ensure goods are compliant with technical regulations before they depart the UK"). Similar agreements have also been signed with New Zealand and Australia.[34] UK authorities have also engaged in joint inspections for good clinical practice (GCP) with their Canadian and US counterparts (Health Canada and USFDA).

In addition, the country has concluded MoUs with several countries. These generally cover the exchange of information (e.g. on clinical trials, compliance, etc.) under a confidentiality agreement. MoUs are not legally binding but help to build trust relationships that may lead to the conclusion of an MRA. In 2018, MHRA signed an MoU with the China Food and Drug Administration (CFDA) that expands on the previous one signed in 2014 (focused on the exchange of safety information on medicines and medical devices). The new agreement is of particular interest in that it "pledges new areas of co-operation such as an exchange of learning from the accelerated access review (AAR) and how to effectively regulate the trading of medicines online".[35]

Early 2019 MHRA signed an MoU with its Russian counterpart. In addition to the exchange of information on medicines regulations and safety issues, this MoU foresees co-operation on Good Manufacturing Practice (GMP) inspections as well as on enforcement activities.[36]

MHRA's bilateral regulatory co-operation agreements are presented in Table 4.4.

### Table 4.4. MHRA's bilateral regulatory co-operation agreements

| MoUs | Confidentiality agreements |
| --- | --- |
| CFDA (China) | FDA (USA) |
| CDSCO (India) | ANVISA (Brazil) |
| FDA (USA) | Medsafe (New Zealand) |
| TGA (Australia) | HPFB (Canada) |
| HAS (Singapore) | FDA (Ghana) |
| Swissmedic (Switzerland) | PMDA (Japan) |
| KNIH (South Korea) | KMA (Kosovo) |
| DKMA (Denmark) | COFEPRIS (Mexico) |
| HPRA (Ireland) | MFDS (South Korea) |
| State Institute of Drugs and Good Practices of the Ministry of Industry and Trade of the Russian Federation (Russia) [on GMP inspections only] | |

Source: MHRA.

### *Engagement in regional or international bodies / initiatives*

Whilst a member of the EU, the United Kingdom, via MHRA, was part of the European Medicines Agency (EMA),[37] which encompasses over fifty national regulatory authorities for human and veterinary medicines in the European Economic Area. The EMA, whose offices moved from London to Amsterdam ahead of the withdrawal from the EU (pharmaceuticals regulation should be done in a member state), is at the network's core. UK experts participated in EMA's scientific committees, working parties and other groups, including multinational assessment teams for marketing authorisation applications and post-authorisation applications to extend existing marketing authorisations.[38] In the same vein, the United Kingdom was part of the EU Pharmacovigilance Risk Assessment Committee and had access to the EudraVigilance system for managing and analysing information on suspected adverse reactions to medicines authorised in the EEA.[39] Moreover, MHRA was part of the National Competent Authority Report Exchange, which serves to share safety information on medical devices across the EU.

As part of the EU delegation, the UK participated in the International Council on Harmonisation of Technical Requirements for Registration of Pharmaceuticals for Human Use (ICH). This organisation, which brings together the regulatory bodies of the EU, the US and Japan as well as representatives from the pharmaceutical industry, works to harmonise medicines registration globally. Its Council issues guidelines on requirements for medicines registration that, while not legally binding, are extensively applied in member jurisdictions (as ICH regulators commit to implementing them[40]). In addition to being part of the EU delegation, the UK played a role in several ICH expert working groups.

Since 1999, MHRA is also a member of the Pharmaceutical Inspection Co-operation Scheme (PIC/S), which is a network of Regulatory Authorities in the field of Good Manufacturing Practice (GMP) of medicinal products for human or veterinary use. It comprises 52 participating authorities from across the world (Europe, Africa, America, Asia and Australasia). "PIC/S aims at harmonising inspection procedures worldwide by developing common standards in the field of GMP and by providing training opportunities to inspectors. It also aims at facilitating co-operation and networking between competent authorities, regional and international organisations, thus increasing mutual confidence".[41]

As an OECD member country, the United Kingdom participates, via MHRA, in the OECD's Working Group on Good Laboratory Practice (GLP), which also covers other product categories such as chemicals. The Group notably seeks to ensure that test data have been generated in accordance with the organisation's GLP principles. To do so, it aims at facilitating information exchanges among monitoring authorities to avoid duplication, allow an efficient allocation of resources and ensure adequate compliance monitoring (harmonising testing procedures for the Mutual Acceptance of Data, or MAD).[42]

Moreover, the United Kingdom is a member of the International Coalition of Medicines Regulatory Authorities (ICMRA), which aims at addressing "current and emerging human medicine regulatory and safety challenges globally".[43] UK authorities also engage in co-operation on bioequivalence studies as part of the work of the World Health Organisation to issue international guidance in this area.[44]

### Outstanding challenges

Continued alignment with European regulations and associated networks appears to be critical for the supply of safe and effective medicines and medical devices to the United Kingdom, as well as for appropriate monitoring and market surveillance and continuity of business in the country's pharmaceutical sector. In March 2018, the UK's Health and Social Care Select Committee did indeed call on the government to secure "the closest possible regulatory alignment with the EU on medicines and medical devices regulation". Other potential withdrawal-related risks include delays in the detection and management for pharmacovigilance, loss of the UK's influence in the ICH, and delays in accessing specific types of medicines (e.g. for rare diseases).[45]

The UK Government has in turn repeatedly stated its willingness to pursue a close relationship with EMA as well as the EU regulatory network on medicines and medical device regulation. While continued membership does not seem to be an option for the time being (no provisions exist for third countries to become members or observers at the EMA), existing agreements between the EMA and third countries such as Switzerland, the US and Canada could be models worth considering.

## Product safety

The UK Government and regulatory authorities have acknowledged the importance of IRC for product safety in their strategic policy planning, in particular its role in building consumer confidence, reducing the cost and complexity for industry and consumers, and facilitating cross-border market access.

As a member of the EU, the country heavily relied on the standards, common regulatory approaches (under the General Product Safety Directive and the New Legislative Framework[46]) and market surveillance infrastructure for product safety provided by the EU. Appropriate action is needed for the country's product safety regime to function properly following withdrawal from the EU. Among other impacts, the withdrawal means that the results of conformity assessment carried out by UK conformity assessment bodies are no longer recognised in the EU, and the United Kingdom is no longer able to participate in either the EU's Safety Gate rapid alert system or the Information and Communication System on Market Surveillance (although the Government have taken steps to mitigate against the potential loss of access to EU-level data).

Given the uncertainty regarding the UK's future relationship with the EU, there is a need to explore all potential IRC venues, either bilaterally (e.g. in the form of mutual recognition agreements) or multilaterally. This need is made all the more critical that the rapidly changing technological environment is putting pressure on regulators and enforcers.

## *Main rationale for international regulatory co-operation in the sector*

With the development of the EU single market, the EU acquis and UK law in the area of consumer protection, including consumer product safety, became increasingly interwoven (House of Lords, 2017[9]). The UK's current product safety and metrology regime is based mostly on EU legislation, so as to enable the free trade of goods which meet EU-wide product safety and metrology specifications and mutual recognition for accredited bodies.[47]

A 2017 report by the House of Lords highlights the benefits from the EU acquis in this area. It provides a harmonised framework that strengthens the legal protection of citizens. It facilitates information sharing so cross-border problems can be "tackled at both ends". It facilitates market surveillance and the enforcement of trading standards through investment in enabling infrastructure – the Safety Gate rapid alert system being a case in point.

Following the UK withdrawal from the EU, the results of conformity assessment carried out by UK conformity assessment bodies are no longer recognised in the EU. As a result, products due to be placed on the EU market need to be assessed by an EU recognised conformity assessment body.[48] Given, the importance of the EU as an export market as well as of the consumer products category (it accounts for about one-quarter of trade in goods worldwide) (UNCTAD, 2019[10]), the United Kingdom needs to ensure that its domestic legal framework in this area remains interoperable with the EU and endowed with suitable enforcement mechanisms. This perspective raises the critical importance that IRC will take in the future.

The importance of IRC has been acknowledged in OPSS' 2018-2020 Strategy for strengthening national capacity for product safety. The Strategy states the UK's willingness "to remain at the leading edge of regulatory innovation through participation and leadership of international networks as well as working with the EU, OECD and other partners to address pan-European and global safety risks". The Strategy highlights the role of European and international standards in building consumer confidence and providing a clear framework against which businesses can achieve and demonstrate compliance. It also acknowledges that "common standards greatly reduce the cost and complexity for industry and consumers, enable business to operate easily across borders and simplify market access".

IRC is also becoming increasingly important in the areas of enforcement and market surveillance given the emergence and increasing market power of new categories of actors that span across jurisdictions (e.g. online platforms) as well as the need to respond in a co-ordinated fashion to the questions raised by rapid technological change and product innovation.

### UK bodies involved

The Office for Product Safety and Standards (OPSS),[49] which was created in 2018 and is part of BEIS, oversees the regulatory system for product safety and standards in the UK. Its remit covers general (non-food) consumer product safety such as white goods, electrical goods, toys, clothes and cosmetics, except for areas where national capability and regulators already exist (e.g. vehicles, medicines and medical devices, workplace equipment).[50] OPSS's website highlights the Office's efforts in support of operational best practice and co-ordination of local regulation of product safety and metrology. It also highlights, as part of its core functions, how OPSS works to share its expertise in this area domestically as well as internationally.

### Product safety under the EU

EU rules on product safety are defined in the New Legislative Framework as well as in the General Product Safety Directive. Under the Directive, a product is safe if it meets all essential safety requirements under European or national law. If there are no regulations or European standards, the product's compliance is determined according to other reference documents such as national standards, Commission recommendations, codes of practice, etc.[51]

Regulatory co-operation in the EU/EEA area is particularly strong in the area of market surveillance. The Safety Gate rapid alert system[52] (also known as RAPEX) and its associated database is a cornerstone in this regard. It enables quick exchange of information between countries and with the European Commission about dangerous non-food products posing a risk to the health and safety of consumers.[53] Beyond the EU, the Information and Communication System on Market Surveillance (ICSMS) provides an IT platform for communication between EU and EFTA market surveillance bodies on non-compliant products. It aims to avoid the duplication of work ("as it records both compliant and non-compliant products, scarce resources can be optimised by not undertaking testing/sampling on products previously found compliant by other surveillance authorities").[54] It also speeds up the removal of unsafe products from the market.[55]

Under this framework, OPSS aims at ensuring that all relevant international standards are taken into account in UK legislation as much as possible. OPSS also has responsibility for specific UK domestic legislation e.g. furniture and fire safety. While the United Kingdom was a member of the EU, OPSS was also the UK's national contact point for the EU market surveillance system, under which the Commission published a weekly summary of alerts reported to it by the relevant national authorities (e.g. local authorities and national trading standards bodies). This included information on the dangerous products found, associated risks and any measures taken in the notifying country to prevent or restrict their marketing or use (House of Lords, 2017, p. 14[9]).

The UK authorities have acknowledged that, without action (e.g. to convert EU-derived product safety and metrology legislation into UK law), the withdrawal from the EU threatens the country's current product safety regime. This has implications for consumer protection as well as business continuity.[56] The UK government has expressed its willingness to retain access to both Safety Gate and ICSMS following the withdrawal. OPSS has also taken steps to develop its own product safety database.

### IRC beyond the EU

While the United Kingdom was a member of the EU, its regulatory co-operation at the bilateral level (i.e. with jurisdictions beyond Europe) in the product safety field was conditioned by its participation in the EU single market: once a product was lawfully placed on the market in one member state, it could be marketed in any member state without barriers – subject to some limited exceptions (Webb and Wright, 2018[11]). This de facto meant that any bilateral agreement had larger implications than for the United Kingdom only.

One referent of the co-operation between the EU and non-EU partners can be found in the EEA model. In order to allow access to the EU single market, this model requires that the parties replace their national laws on product safety with the harmonised European laws on product requirements. Similarly, enhanced mutual recognition agreements (MRAs), which are based on an alignment with EU rules, currently exist between the EU and Israel, Switzerland and Turkey. The EU also has MRAs with Australia, Israel, New Zealand and the US, as well as with Canada, Japan and South Korea (within the context of their respective FTAs). These tend however to be narrower in scope (e.g. limited to conformity testing in the case of the MRA with the US) (Webb and Wright, 2018[11]).

After leaving the European Union, the United Kingdom may have to engage more extensively in greater IRC, both at the bilateral and the multilateral levels, to compensate for the possible loss in trade and the safety risks raised. The country has recently concluded bilateral MRAs on conformity assessment with the United States, Australia and New Zealand to ensure continuity of trade once the current agreements that those countries have with the EU cease to apply to the United Kingdom.

The OPSS also maintains a Technical Assistance Programme, through its Regulatory Delivery International team, which provides technical advice to developing countries in order to promote the reform or design of regulations, laws and strategies. The team works with other government departments with an international focus, including DIT, DFID and through the FCO Prosperity Fund.[57] Recent examples of these projects have included working with the Government of Indonesia to put into place systems for improved central oversight and co-ordination of regulatory reform.

OPSS sponsors the British Standards Institution (BSI), which is a member of the International Organization for Standardization (ISO) as well as the International Electrotechnical Commission (IEC).[58] In this context, OPSS is involved in committee meetings for standard development but does not have a primary role. Its work focuses, according to consulted officials, on making the international standard-setting process more inclusive, for example by encouraging BSI to take into account the needs of those ultimately affected by the standards, including in the civil society. In addition, the United Kingdom Accreditation Service (UKAS) is a member of the International Accreditation Forum (IAF), the world association of Conformity Assessment Accreditation Bodies,[59] and a signatory of the Mutual Recognition Arrangement under the International Laboratory Accreditation Cooperation (ILAC).[60]

## *Outstanding challenges*

The modalities of agreement between the United Kingdom and the EU remain uncertain, and the United Kingdom may no longer be able to participate in either the EU's Safety Gate rapid alert system or ICSMS, which are critical for effective and efficient market surveillance. As the effectiveness of market surveillance activity relies on intelligence, any reduction in available sources of information will have an impact on how market surveillance is targeted. The potential resource implications of such a scenario need to be considered alongside the ongoing reduction in trading standards services, which, according to the Chartered Trading Standards Institute (CTSI) of the UK, "severely limits the UK's ability to meet the government's aim for robust market surveillance in the post-Brexit market for goods" (Ctsi, 2018[12]).

CTSI also points to the implications of the UK's withdrawal from EU legislation networks; e.g. risks of losing out in networking and events such as the Product Safety Week and at Consumer Safety Network meetings. This may in turn result in a loss of expertise and knowledge and could lead to an inconsistent application of relevant EU legislation. In the same vein, the withdrawal from the EU may lead to a gradual deviation in the long term between UK product-related regulations and the EU legal framework in this area.[61]

With the multiplication of bilateral trade and sector agreements with key partners beyond the EU, the United Kingdom may find itself in a difficult situation of having to balance preserving access to the EU single market and accommodating other jurisdictions' regulations. A general approach may be difficult to maintain in this context, which may be easier to manage through a sector-by-sector policy depending on market shares (i.e. UK's overall dependence on EU vs. other markets).

Strong IRC, including on enforcement, will also be important for the UK to address emerging challenges, such as the expansion of e-commerce (including cross-border) and online platforms and the increasingly fast pace of technological change and product innovation.

## References

BEIS (2018), *Euratom Exit Factsheet: Nuclear Cooperation Agreement*, https://assets.publishing.service.gov.uk/government/uploads/system/uploads/attachment_data/file/717194/euratom-exit-factsheet-nuclear-cooperation-agreement.pdf. [6]

Ctsi (2018), *CTSI Brexit Think Tank Trading Standards Opportunities and Threats from the UK Withdrawal from the EU*, http://www.journaloftradingstandards.co.uk/wp-content/uploads/2018/11/CTSI_Brexit_Think_Tank_Full_Report.pdf (accessed on 24 October 2019). [12]

HM Treasury (2019), *Financial Services Future Review: Call for Evidence*, https://assets.publishing.service.gov.uk/government/uploads/system/uploads/attachment_data/file/819025/Future_Regulatory_Framework_Review_Call_for_Evidence.pdf (accessed on 15 July 2018). [3]

House of Commons (2019), "Brexit and medicines", *Briefing Paper*, Vol. 8148, https://researchbriefings.files.parliament.uk/documents/CBP-8148/CBP-8148.pdf. [8]

House of Lords (2017), "Brexit: will consumers be protected?", *HL Paper 51*, https://publications.parliament.uk/pa/ld201719/ldselect/ldeucom/51/51.pdf. [9]

NS Energy (2018), *Exiting Euratom: Renegotiating the UK's role in Europe's nuclear family*, https://www.nsenergybusiness.com/news/euratom-brexit-uk-nuclear/ (accessed on 24 October 2019). [7]

ONR (2019), *ONR Strategic Framework for International Engagement to 2025*, Office of Nuclear Regulation, http://www.onr.org.uk/documents/2019/onr-strategic-framework-for-international-engagement.pdf. [4]

ONR (2019), *ONR Strategic Framework for International Engagement to 2025*, http://www.onr.org.uk/documents/2019/onr-strategic-framework-for-international-engagement.pdf. [5]

Rhodes, C. (2019), "Financial services: contribution to the UK economy", *House of Commons Library*, Vol. 6193, https://researchbriefings.files.parliament.uk/documents/SN06193/SN06193.pdf. [1]

TheCityUK (2018), *Key facts about the UK as an international financial centre 2018*, https://www.thecityuk.com/assets/2018/Reports-PDF/94053cfc7b/Key-facts-about-the-UK-as-an-international-financial-centre-2018.pdf. [2]

UNCTAD (2019), *Key Statistics and Trends in International Trade 2018*, https://unctad.org/en/PublicationsLibrary/ditctab2019d2_en.pdf. [10]

Webb, D. and K. Wright (2018), *Future trade with the EU: Mutual recognition*, House of Commons Library, https://researchbriefings.parliament.uk/ResearchBriefing/Summary/CBP-8384. [11]

## Notes

[1] The UK government and the independent UK regulatory and supervisory authorities have also contributed to shaping the EU regulatory framework (respectively, through negotiations with members States in the Council and discussions in the European Supervisory Authorities. UK members of the European Parliament have also helped shape the Parliament's input to the legislative process.

[2] www.europarl.europa.eu/factsheets/en/sheet/83/financial-services-policy.

[3] This paragraph draws on:
https://www.lexisnexis.com/uk/lexispsl/bankingandfinance/document/391289/5j9y-rdj1-f185-x2my-00000-00/regulatory_architecture_overview00000-00/regulatory_architecture_overview#.

[4] www.bankofengland.co.uk/-/media/boe/files/memoranda-of-understanding/bank-pra-hmt-and-fca-international-organisations.

[5] www.gov.uk/government/news/tenth-economic-and-financial-dialogue-held-between-the-uk-and-china.

[6] www.gov.uk/government/publications/uk-india-9th-economic-and-financial-dialogue-policy-outcomes.

[7] www.gov.uk/government/publications/uk-brazil-3rd-economic-and-financial-dialogue-policy-outcomes.

[8] www.gov.uk/government/publications/joint-statement-us-uk-financial-regulatory-working-group/joint-statement-us-uk-financial-regulatory-working-group.

[9] Id.

[10] www.fca.org.uk/publication/mou/supervisory-mou-fca-sfc.pdf.

[11] www.fca.org.uk/publication/mou/fca-cftc-mou-covered-firms.pdf.

[12] www.fca.org.uk/publication/mou/fsa-mou-rbi.pdf.

[13] www.gov.uk/government/news/dr-liam-fox-launches-new-international-programs-to-boost-uk-fintech-industry.

[14] https://www.fca.org.uk/publication/mou/fsa-mou-rbi.pdf.

[15] www.fsb.org/about/.

[16] www.iosco.org/about/?subSection=mmou&subSection1=signatories.

[17] www.iosco.org/library/pubdocs/pdf/IOSCOPD386.pdf.

[18] www.fatf-gafi.org/about/.

[19] This passage draws heavily on www.fca.org.uk/firms/global-financial-innovation-network.

[20] The FCA launched the Regulatory Sandbox in June 2016. For further information, please see www.fca.org.uk/firms/regulatory-sandbox.

[21] https://assets.publishing.service.gov.uk/government/uploads/system/uploads/attachment_data/file/819025/Future_Regulatory_Framework_Review_Call_for_Evidence.pdf p. 11.

[22] For an overview of these challenges, see www.baselgovernance.org/publications/working-paper-28-regulating-cryptocurrencies-challenges-and-considerations#3.2.

[23] https://publications.parliament.uk/pa/cm201719/cmselect/cmtreasy/910/91002.htm.

[24] https://publications.parliament.uk/pa/cm201719/cmselect/cmtreasy/1845/184502.htm.

[25] See article 80 Withdrawal Agreement, at https://assets.publishing.service.gov.uk/government/uploads/system/uploads/attachment_data/file/840655/Agreement_on_the_withdrawal_of_the_United_Kingdom_of_Great_Britain_and_Northern_Ireland_from_the_European_Union_and_the_European_Atomic_Energy_Community.pdf.

[26] Unless otherwise stated, all direct quotations in this case study refer to this document.

[27] www.onr.org.uk/foi/2018/201810041.htm.

[28] Mostly in the context of the International Atomic Energy Agency's work. ONR's website lists UK representative bodies in each of the four Safety Standards Committees overseen by the Commission on Safety Standards (CSS) as follows:

> NUSSC: Nuclear Safety Standards Committee: National Information Infrastructure (NII)
>
> RASSC: Radiation Safety Standards Committee: NII
>
> WASSC: Radioactive Waste Safety Standards Committee: BEIS
>
> TRANSSC: Safe Transport of Radioactive Material Safety Standards Committee: Department for Transport.
>
> CSS: Commission on Safety Standards: NII Chief Inspector

[29] www.onr.org.uk/agency-agreements-mou.htm.

[30] http://www.gov.uk/government/news/uk-and-russia-sign-mou-on-regulatory-cooperation-on-medicines.

[31] HMRC, UK Trade Info, quoted in (House of Commons, 2019[8])

[32] https://www.ema.europa.eu/en/about-us/how-we-work/european-medicines-regulatory-network.

[33] www.ema.europa.eu/en/documents/other/icmra-mapping-bilateral-arrangements-between-icmra-members_en.pdf.

[34] www.gov.uk/government/news/uk-and-usa-agree-to-continue-mutual-recognition-agreement.

[35] www.gov.uk/government/news/uk-and-china-sign-memorandum-of-understanding-on-medicine-and-device-regulation.

[36] www.gov.uk/government/news/uk-and-russia-sign-mou-on-regulatory-cooperation-on-medicines.

[37] www.ema.europa.eu/en/about-us/how-we-work/european-medicines-regulatory-network.

[38] Idem.

[39] www.ema.europa.eu/en/human-regulatory/overview/pharmacovigilance-overview.

[40] www.ich.org/about/mission.html.

[41] www.picscheme.org/en/about.

[42] www.oecd.org/chemicalsafety/good-laboratory-practiceglp.htm.

[43] www.icmra.info/drupal/en/home.

[44] extranet.who.int/prequal/content/bioequivalence-0.

[45] This paragraph draws extensively on (House of Commons, 2019[8]).

[46] https://ec.europa.eu/growth/single-market/goods/new-legislative-framework_en.

[47] http://www.legislation.gov.uk/ukia/2019/108/pdfs/ukia_20190108_en.pdf.

[48] www.gov.uk/guidance/status-of-conformity-assessment-bodies-after-brexit.

[49] http://www.gov.uk/government/organisations/office-for-product-safety-and-standards.

[50] https://uk.practicallaw.thomsonreuters.com/w-012-7930?transitionType=Default&contextData=(sc.Default)&firstPage=true&bhcp=1.

[51] https://ec.europa.eu/info/business-economy-euro/product-safety-and-requirements/consumer-product-safety/product-safety-rules_en.

[52] https://ec.europa.eu/consumers/consumers_safety/safety_products/rapex/alerts/repository/content/pages/rapex/index_en.htm.

[53] For more details, see: www.gov.uk/government/news/uk-and-usa-agree-to-continue-mutual-recognition-agreement.

[54] http://www.journaloftradingstandards.co.uk/wp-content/uploads/2018/11/ctsi_brexit_think_tank_full_report.pdf.

[55] https://ec.europa.eu/growth/single-market/goods/building-blocks/icsms_en.

[56] www.legislation.gov.uk/ukia/2019/108/pdfs/ukia_20190108_en.pdf.

[57] The primary purpose of the Prosperity Fund is to contribute to the Sustainable Development Goals, agreed at the UN in 2015, through addressing barriers to growth. It does this through improving the global business environment, strengthening institutions, and encouraging greater global private investment. www.gov.uk/government/publications/cross-government-prosperity-fund-programme/cross-government-prosperity-fund-update.

[58] It is also a member of the European Committee for Standardization (CEN) and the European Committee for Electrotechnical Standardization (CENELEC).

[59] www.iaf.nu/.

[60] https://ilac.org/.

[61] Legislation has been introduced to address the short-term concerns in the event of a no-deal withdrawal; e.g. the Product Safety and Metrology etc. (Amendment etc.) (EU Exit) Regulations 2019. For more details, please see www.gov.uk/government/publications/uk-product-safety-and-metrology-guidance-in-a-no-deal-scenario.

# 5 Assessment and recommendations

This chapter builds on the findings of the overall report regarding the context of international regulatory co-operation policies and practices in the United Kingdom, the unilateral efforts undertaken to support regulatory coherence and the co-operative efforts on regulatory matters. It offers three sets of recommendations to the United Kingdom. For a better streamlining of IRC across government, the United Kingdom should build a holistic IRC vision, strategy and strengthen political leadership for IRC with clearly defined roles and responsibilities for key players. To adapt regulations to the global context, the UK should embed IRC more systematically in regulatory management tools and throughout the rule-making cycle. And finally, to facilitate a more systematic use of IRC, it should increase awareness and understanding about IRC across departments and regulators.

# General overview of international regulatory co-operation (IRC) in the United Kingdom

With IRC largely seen as an EU competence to date, the United Kingdom does not have an overarching, cross-government strategic vision and systematic practices on IRC. IRC has mainly been confined to co-operation within the EU, which is strongly framed by specific legal framework and institutions. IRC beyond the EU has been sporadic and sector-specific. Nevertheless, the United Kingdom has a long-standing experience with regulatory policy and strong institutions in place that provide for meaningful opportunities to embed more systematic international considerations in domestic rulemaking and mainstream IRC throughout the rulemaking cycle. As illustrated in Chapter 4, a number of departments and regulators have also developed strong relationships with their peers abroad and as part of their participation in international fora.

## *The legacy*

The United Kingdom has been a leader in promoting the Better Regulation agenda domestically, among EU and OECD members, and beyond. However, IRC is implicitly rather than overtly discussed in its current Better Regulation Framework. It is mainly conducted in an *ad hoc* manner and mostly seen as an EU responsibility. Having said that, the UK's regulatory policy, practices and institutional organisation are strengths upon which to rely to mainstream greater IRC considerations into domestic rulemaking. The strong embedding of specific mechanisms for EU legislation offer in themselves strong entry points for broader IRC considerations.

The UK's request for the OECD to conduct an IRC Review is testament to the country's ambition of ensuring that its IRC processes follow international best practices. It is a unique opportunity for the UK to continue showing leadership on the regulatory policy agenda, in an emerging policy area where most countries are still struggling to establish the basis of the approach.

## *The pressure points*

Technological changes across the globe are making it increasingly challenging for domestic regulators to achieve their core regulatory objectives in isolation. At the same time, integration in global value chains is making the UK economy increasingly interconnected with and dependent on other economies at a global scale, beyond its immediate neighbours. These trends provide meaningful opportunities for a beneficial approach to IRC.

The United Kingdom's withdrawal from the EU is also a strong driver of its IRC efforts. It creates pressure to both move away from and remain aligned to EU regulations, and the UK will need to manage the resulting tensions:

- Building on its years as an EU member, the United Kingdom has both accumulated substantial IRC experience with its neighbouring countries, and delegated a number of regulatory tasks to the EU. With the withdrawal, the mandate of UK departments and regulators is likely to grow with new regulatory responsibilities – the case studies, in particular the ones on product safety and medical products in Chapter 4, provide a prime example and highlights resource implications. This provides an opportunity to embed international considerations in their rulemaking activities more systematically.
- Given geographical proximity and the intensity of flows and current interactions, the United Kingdom will need to maintain close ties with the EU regardless of the modalities of its withdrawal. Interconnectivity of transport, energy and other physical infrastructure will continue driving substantial trans-boundary co-operation. The EU single market is likely to remain the most important trade partner for the United Kingdom. More broadly, the United Kingdom and the EU

have a strong incentive post-withdrawal to collaborate closely to avoid regulatory loopholes and maintain regulatory effectiveness across numerous critical policy areas. The case studies in Chapter 4 highlight the potential weakening of market surveillance and enforcement infrastructure following the withdrawal from the EU. Continuing benefiting from the EU enforcement networks and mechanisms will be particularly critical to preserve regulatory effectiveness.

- The withdrawal also generates strong imperatives for the United Kingdom to collaborate more strongly with countries beyond the EU in order to diversify its partners and compensate for lost co-operation mechanisms and related privileges. There are co-operation opportunities both bilaterally, plurilaterally and through more active engagement in multilateral international organisations (IOs). The Better Regulation Framework and the past experience of integrating past EU legislation into the UK's regulatory framework provide opportunities and entry points to embed broader IRC considerations in UK rulemaking.
- With the withdrawal from the EU, the United Kingdom may lose the benefit of acting through a bigger bloc of countries in a number of international co-operation initiatives. This position still offers many co-operation opportunities but may make bilateral relations costlier for the United Kingdom. Where bilateral or regional co-operation is critical – i.e. for issues and in sectors where there is strong bilateral or regional ties and geographic proximity matters significantly – the consequence for the United Kingdom may be a certain level of unilateral adoption of the partner's approach. For issues requiring multilateral solutions, channelling the UK's agenda through international fora (where one country equals one vote or decision is consensus based – regardless of size) or through coalitions of like-minded countries may be more cost effective.

## Key priority areas of focus for the United Kingdom on IRC

Whatever the future relation with the EU, the UK regulatory framework would gain from a stronger systematic consideration of the international environment. This involves: i) building a holistic IRC vision and strategy with clearly defined roles and responsibilities; ii) embedding stronger IRC considerations in regulatory management tools (beyond trade and business impacts) and throughout the rulemaking cycle; and iii) updating incentives, awareness and guidance to departments and regulators.

### *Building a holistic IRC vision, a strategy and political leadership for IRC in the United Kingdom, with clearly defined roles and responsibilities for key players, to develop quality regulation in a globalised context*

*Assessment*

IRC initiatives in the United Kingdom (beyond those related to the EU framework) are largely fragmented and sector-specific. Whilst there are references to the importance of gathering evidence from international best practice in certain pieces of guidance, including in the HM Treasury Green Book, the main efforts currently undertaken to enhance IRC is in the trade area. This is illustrated by the introduction of a new trade question in the RIA template and related notifications to the World Trade Organization (WTO).

However, IRC is not a purely trade facilitating tool: it has important broader benefits for policy makers, regulators and society, for example via learning from peers abroad, or aligning approaches on common and cross-border policy challenges to strengthen the effectiveness of domestic regulation in achieving its policy objectives. Co-operation is also a cornerstone of effective market surveillance and regulatory enforcement. With the growing dematerialisation of flows transcending borders, regulatory co-operation across different jurisdictions is becoming critical to the identification of non-compliant behaviours, the detection of dangerous products and their remedies. From this perspective, IRC may help achieve other broader objectives such as safety, social and environmental.

The United Kingdom has a strong system of centralised oversight on better regulation. Responsibility for oversight is shared between the Better Regulation Executive (BRE), which develops the framework and guidance for better regulation and the Regulatory Policy Committee (RPC), which provides external, independent scrutiny of evidence and analysis supporting RIAs and *ex post* evaluations of legislation. This allows these bodies to provide strategic leadership on better regulation, offer guidance and support on all matters related to better regulation and ensure independent scrutiny of better regulation efforts across regulatory initiatives. The Better Regulation Units (BRUs) play an important role in embedding the better regulation agenda across Government Departments. However, IRC is not an explicit area of oversight in the Better Regulation Framework, and relevant tasks are split across a number of bodies, including mainly the BRE, the RPC, the Foreign and Commonwealth Office (FCO) and the Department for International Trade (DIT). Departments and regulatory agencies are key implementers of IRC. This multiplicity of actors involved in the oversight and conduct of IRC, and the lack of incentive for these bodies to work together in a co-ordinated way, results in an *ad hoc* and case-by-case approach to IRC.

The United Kingdom is taking many measures to prepare for being outside the EU in order to avoid major impacts of the withdrawal for its businesses and citizens. It is pursuing new IRC opportunities globally (e.g. through continuity agreements and regulatory diplomacy for example). The United Kingdom would benefit from a stronger common IRC thread throughout these initiatives, guided by a whole-of-government policy. This would also involve making explicit the IRC considerations which may be currently implicitly contained in the various components of the better regulation agenda. Nonetheless, the political economy of IRC in a post-withdrawal context will not be easy to manage. While stronger IRC policies may be called for to compensate for the loss of EU mechanisms, it should be recognised that certain stronger forms of IRC may limit a country's regulatory space and sovereignty and attract political controversy.

In this context, a narrative identifying the rationale and benefits of IRC will be important. There are many examples of how such co-operation has benefitted governments, regulators, business and citizens.[1] The regulatory challenges of emerging technologies in particular provide a strong rationale for IRC. The Government's June 2019 White Paper, "Regulation for the Fourth Industrial Revolution"[2] illustrates these challenges and delineates a long-term plan to reform the UK's approach to regulating technological innovation. It highlights existing work and sets out a number of proposals, which have the potential to strengthen the use of IRC in policymaking.

*Recommendations*

- Ensure IRC leadership and systematic mainstreaming from the Government institutions responsible for better regulation policy and oversight. To have maximum impact, strong IRC leadership should sit with part of government with sufficient cross-government oversight of cross-sectoral regulatory activity, ideally a committee of ministers to provide political leadership. Examples of such parts of Government that have exhibited these qualities could include the Ministerial Working Group on Future Regulation, tasked with overseeing the implementation of the White Paper reforms (Box 1.5) or the (now abolished) Reducing Regulation Sub-Committee (Box 1.4).
- Sufficient financial and human resources should be dedicated to ensuring the systematic application of IRC rules within departments. IRC is part and parcel of the regulatory policy agenda – it is an important building block of regulatory quality. As such, there should be dedicated staff strongly connected to the Better Regulation agenda and Framework with sufficient resources and influence to ensure maximum mainstreaming in the rulemaking practices of departments and regulators.

- Roles and responsibilities on IRC policy and oversight should be clearly defined and close co-operation fostered between the various institutions involved (the BRE, the RPC, the BRUs, the FCO and DIT) to ensure that IRC efforts resonate with regulators. On this, the experience from Canada and New Zealand provides reference points (Box 5.1).
- The BRE and RPC, as oversight bodies for the better regulation framework, should play an active role in pushing forward and mainstreaming the IRC agenda. They should work closely with the BRUs and the wider analytical community and Board Level Champions, to ensure that they have sufficiently detailed technical understanding of IRC, thereby enabling them to challenge their respective departments to integrate IRC into policymaking processes.
- Develop a whole-of-government strategy, with a single, broad, definition of IRC and common public policy objectives in line with the UK Government's strategic priorities, taking into account Government departments, regulatory bodies and the devolved administrations. In particular, take into consideration the potential of IRC to pursue regulatory objectives including social and environmental objectives, while also taking into account its benefits for facilitating international trade.
- The part of government tasked with developing the IRC Strategy must ensure that it is shared across government and designed with inputs from within and outside of government to ensure ownership of the government's IRC priorities. Regulators know their field and peers. The government objective should be to facilitate their co-operation by clarifying what IRC is and what can be expected from it; and to provide guidance where needed, by facilitating access to the relevant information.
- Take forward the White Paper proposals and monitor their implementation, as these contain a number of proposals, which could help build UK IRC capacity at a number of levels. These include building methodologies and understanding of the effects of regulation on trade amongst departments/regulators; ensuring that IRC is reflected in trade deals and working upstream to influence IRC in international fora. However, it is crucial that IRC is not viewed solely through a trade lens and the government IRC Strategy also reflects the potential for IRC to align approaches on common and cross-border policy challenges e.g. working closely together to ensure the continued effectiveness of environmental regulatory frameworks relating to air quality and climate change
- While it is important that the strategic vision supports the transition in the withdrawal from the EU, this vision should be long-term and well rooted into the better regulation agenda. In particular, this involves preventing the UK IRC and regulatory policy agendas more broadly from becoming merely a response to the UK's withdrawal from the EU and ensuring that they remain state-of-the-art and forward looking.
- As the UK develops its IRC policy, it should be targeted/focused proportionately upon aspects of economic activity with the largest regulatory impact. It should give priority to key partners for collaboration, taking into account the UK's degree of "dependence" on other countries, depend on sectors and account for IRC drivers (Box 5.2). Given the geographic proximity and historic links, it is likely to entail maintaining close ties with the EU.
- As Departments implement the new "trade" impact of the RIA / ex-post review processes, it will provide valuable data to feed into the IRC Strategy, inform on areas of priority and potential IRC partners, and support upstream trade negotiations. The case of Norway can also usefully inform UK policy makers on how relate to the EU legislation as a non-member, both to influence and then adopt / implement it (Box 5.3).
- The United Kingdom should leverage further its strong record in regulatory policy to promote good regulatory practices, including IRC, internationally. A strong culture of regulatory quality allows better dialogue on regulatory matters and facilitate the development of trust across governments and regulators.

### Box 5.1. Whole of government strategy and organisation of IRC: experiences from Canada and New Zealand

**Canada**

IRC is formally embedded in Canada's overarching regulatory policy framework, the Cabinet Directive on Regulation (CDR). The CDR requires regulators to assess opportunities for co-operation and alignment with other jurisdictions, domestically and internationally, in order to reduce unnecessary regulatory burden on Canadian businesses while maintaining or improving the health, safety, security, social and economic well-being of Canadians, and protecting the environment. Where a Canada-specific approach is required, regulators must provide a rationale in the regulatory impact assessment statement.

The Government of Canada has a dedicated team responsible for supporting and co-ordinating efforts to foster international and domestic regulatory co-operation. This team sits within the central regulatory oversight body, the Treasury Board Secretariat of Canada (TBS). In Budget 2019, the TBS was granted permanent funding covering 16 full-time employees to co-ordinate domestic and international regulatory co-operation efforts, including management, policy, sector analysts and administrative support.

The team's activities include working with regulators to ensure that they meet their obligations under the CDR, as well as leading Canada's participation in three formal regulatory co-operation mechanisms: the Canada-European Union Comprehensive Economic and Trade Agreement Regulatory Cooperation Forum, the Canada-United States Regulatory Cooperation Council and the domestic Federal-Provincial/Territorial Regulatory Reconciliation and Cooperation Table under the Canadian Free Trade Agreement. TBS works with Canadian federal regulators, as with officials in the United States, the European Union, and provinces/territories, to reduce unnecessary regulatory differences and eliminate duplicative requirements and barriers between jurisdictions. TBS also works closely with Global Affairs Canada to negotiate regulatory provisions in trade agreements, including those related to IRC.

**New Zealand**

In New Zealand, IRC considerations are embedded in core documents, including the Government Expectations for Good Regulatory Practice and the Government's Regulatory Management Strategy: Building Effective Regulatory Institutions and Practices. Responsibility for oversight and promoting consideration of IRC is shared across several agencies.

The Regulatory Quality Team within the Treasury, a central agency, exercises stewardship over the regulatory management system to maintain and enhance the quality of government-initiated regulation. This team is the lead agency on good regulatory practice for New Zealand.

The Ministry of Business, Innovation and Employment (MBIE), takes the lead on promoting international regulatory coherence, which includes promoting international regulatory co-operation in its many forms. MBIE and Treasury work in close collaboration and are both involved in the negotiation and implementation of cross-cutting GRP and regulatory co-operation chapters in FTAs. Treasury and MBIE share responsibility for representing New Zealand at international regulatory policy fora, and co-ordinating New Zealand's contribution to benchmarking studies of regulation and the regulatory environment.

The Ministry of Foreign Affairs and Trade is New Zealand's lead advisor and negotiator on trade policy. The Ministry oversees and provides advice on the process by which the New Zealand Government enters into treaties.

## Box 5.2. The IRC drivers

OECD has identified a number of factors that promote, hinder and shape IRC endeavours. These hypotheses may inform policymakers pondering about when, how and with whom to engage in IRC. They do not represent, however, static rules on the political economy of IRC.

- Geographical proximity: geographical proximity may increase the need and likelihood of co-operation and IRC due to joint challenges, similar worldviews and preferences.
- Economic interdependence: high trade volumes may increase the likelihood for co-operation so as to lock in a certain level of regulatory openness and to lower trade costs through the dismantling of unnecessary regulatory divergence. Balanced interdependence should moreover promote the use of negotiated IRC instruments, while imbalanced interdependence should promote the use of unilateral IRC instruments such as Good Regulatory Practices (GRP).
- Political and economic properties of potential partners: IRC should be easier in hierarchical relationships between rule-makers and rule-takers than in hierarchical relationships between two rule-makers or two rule-takers. In non-hierarchical complex relationships, the availability of international regulation and standards should significantly facilitate IRC.
- Nature of regulation: the political sensitivity of measures subject to regulation – i.e. their inherent risk levels or social and economic nature – should significantly affect the likelihood of IRC. IRC on politically sensitive measures should be more difficult than IRC on less sensitive measures. IRC commitments, moreover, can promote market integration on a preferential basis or non-preferential basis. Preferential commitments should fuel competitive IRC efforts, whereas non-preferential IRC should trigger no such phenomenon. Finally, depending on the sector, regulation and standards can be subject to either positive feedback processes promoting IRC or inter-state competition and free riding dynamics hindering IRC.
- Domestic regulatory governance: IRC may hinge on transparent regulatory governance and the ability of states to actually enforce regulation and IRC commitments at the domestic level.

Source: Basedow and Kauffmann (2016), "The Political Economy of International Regulatory Co-operation: A theoretical framework to understand international regulatory co-operation", OECD, Paris, unpublished Working Paper.

## Box 5.3. Norway adoption and implementation of EU legislation

The European Economic Area (EEA) brings together the EU member states and three of the European Free Trade Association (EFTA) States (Iceland, Liechtenstein and Norway). It was established by the EEA Agreement in 1992 and enables these three EFTA States to participate fully in the Single Market. The EEA represents a tight and elaborate IRC system with one big and three small partners. In Norway, the formal decision-making process covers the EEA Agreement and the agreements with the EU in the field of justice and home affairs.

The EEA Committee must first make a decision to incorporate new EU legal acts into the EEA Agreement before they can be implemented in Norwegian law through legislative or regulatory decisions.

> The government can implement most of the legal acts from the EEA agreement in Norway, but legislative acts must be submitted to the Norwegian parliament (The Storting) if they entail amendments to the law, financial obligations or are considered of particular importance. Due to the principle of uniform development of the regulations in the EEA, an EU legal act should in principle be implemented and come into effect simultaneously throughout the EEA.
>
> The EEA Agreement does not include participation in the EU's decision-making process. It provides, however, the opportunity to observe and participate in an early stage, i.e. when the European Commission (EC)'s proposal is being formulated. The possibilities of being heard for Norway as an EEA-member when the process in the EU is approaching decisions are more limited.
>
> In the preparatory phase of new regulations, Norway has the right to participate in expert groups and committees under the Commission. Expert groups are forums consulted by the EC on a free and informal basis in the preparation of proposals for new regulations. Norwegian experts participate on an equal footing with experts from the member states. The purpose is to strengthen the academic basis for the EC's work. The EC is not bound by their views and recommendations and there is therefore no requirement for them to arrive at a common position.
>
> The EU also has a number of formal committees consisting of representatives of national authorities who assist the EC in the work on supplementary regulations. The committees have a formal role in the EU's decision-making process. This is where the regulations governing the implementation of directives and regulations adopted by the European Parliament and the Council are being prepared. Norway has only observer status and cannot participate in voting.
>
> Norwegian ministries and regulatory bodies spend substantial time and resources on following EU regulatory work in all stages. There is a large Norwegian representation with the EC staffed with diplomats and sector specialists. In addition, many regulators spend significant time travelling to Brussels in the preparatory phase of new EU regulation.

## Embed IRC more systematically in regulatory management tools and throughout the rulemaking cycle

### Assessment

IRC is implicit rather than explicit in the UK Better Regulation Framework and related regulatory policy tools and disciplines, resulting in case by case IRC practices by departments and regulators. There are some references to the importance of considering international evidence in the HM Treasury Green Book. However, IRC is de facto mainly promoted in the Better Regulation Framework from a trade facilitation perspective: through the consideration of international standards (which are exempt from the Business Impact Target if implemented via non-regulatory means – an implicit requirement) and the introduction of a trade question in the RIA template.

Supposedly, the RIA process is an opportunity for the gathering of overseas / international intelligence and expertise by departments. However, because of the strong focus of the Better Regulation Framework on regulatory burdens on businesses (driven by the provisions of the SBEE Act that introduced the Business Impact Target), departments and regulators tend to focus on the regulatory costs to business, rather than on the quality of the narrative and the evidence provided in the analysis. In any case, IRC is not particularly considered in the cost / benefit assessment of the RIA processes, or in the BIT assessments that both departments and regulators must undertake.

IRC also is not yet sufficiently embedded into the UK Government's Post-Implementation Review (PIR) processes, or in the specific regulators' evaluation processes. The SBEE Act does establish a duty on departments to review regulatory provisions in secondary legislation, which implement EU or international obligations, and to consider if there would be better ways of delivering these changes.[3] However, the various guidance documents, including the Better Regulation Framework Guidance, PIR Guidance and the PIR template do not include a requirement for departments to consider to what extent regulation has been consistent with or has departed from international instruments and practices and whether its delivery has had cross border unintended consequences. Departments have nevertheless been so far directed to identify how UK's implementation of EU measures compares with other EU member states, which provides an important opportunity and entry point to broaden the requirement beyond the EU.

In addition, international expertise and the relevance of foreign or international frameworks for domestic regulatory purposes remains largely undervalued overall (despite the fact that HMT's Green Book points to the need for consideration of international comparators to form part of analysis). There is no specific promotion of IRC in the Better Regulation Framework Guidance. Whilst the RPC reports considering and promoting the use of international evidence as part of its scrutiny of the robustness of the analysis underlying RIAs, it is unclear how much of an incentive this implicit focus provides to departments. In addition, the existence of a de minimis threshold, with the aim of focusing scrutiny on the highest impact measures, has reduced the number of RIAs scrutinised by the RPC. The proposals falling under the threshold still undergo a degree of scrutiny in their development process, e.g. chief analyst signing off, the interdepartmental collective agreement process and parliamentary scrutiny. However, these are not likely to promote IRC given its largely implicit nature in the Better Regulation Framework.

*Recommendations*

IRC should be better embedded in policy tools throughout the rulemaking cycle in order to guarantee that they are genuinely and systematically considered by UK departments and regulators. This implies that the Government should:

- If possible, update the relevant legislation and policy documents, which frame regulatory policy to embed IRC and to ensure that departments and regulators have any necessary legal mandate to undertake such activities. The Government may wish to review whether the SBEE Act provisions regarding the Business Impact Target affect the incentives of departments and regulators to consider IRC when assessing the impact of new regulatory measures. Should the UK Government consider revising the legal requirements around Better Regulation post EU withdrawal, this would provide an opportunity to embed a broader vision of regulatory quality via either legislation or administrative rules. IRC should then be considered on the same level as the other key high-level principles driving regulatory quality, as provided by the 2012 OECD Recommendation on Regulatory Policy and Governance (OECD, 2012[1]).

- Modify policy guidance on regulatory policy, including the Better Regulation Framework Guidance and other key sources of guidance (e.g. HMT Green Book) to embed explicit recommendations to consider the international environment and to help departments and regulators understand how and when to consider IRC in the regulatory process. It will also be important to consider whether the UK Regulators' Code needs updating to ensure that regulators are considering IRC in their analytical processes. Canada and New Zealand provide examples of how to embed IRC in the traditional regulatory management tools (Box 5.4).

- Clarify and emphasise the importance of considering the extent to which new regulations are compatible with existing EU, foreign and international evidence, regulatory options and experiences in the Better Regulation Framework, in the related guidance, and in the criteria used by the RPC for analysing RIAs. In particular, the use of relevant foreign and international evidence could be explicitly mentioned as being an important element of quality evidence to be used in RIA and PIR. Systematic references to international practices in the same field could be encouraged as part of the policy development for any new regulatory measure and the reasons for departing from them explained (even for those measures under the de minimis threshold). Box 5 provides examples of requirement to consider international standards and other relevant regulatory frameworks in other jurisdictions.

- Provide departments and regulators methodological help to consider IRC in the cost and benefit calculation for the BIT. As an example, Canada has introduced IRC as a credit in the "one-in, one-out" exercise (Box 5.6).
- The Government should consider whether regulatory bodies have sufficient resourcing to increase their level of IRC activities. IRC is not a cost-free activity and adequate resources will be a critical success factor in their ability to systematically embed IRC in their rule making processes. Ultimately, there are efficiency and effectiveness gains of regulatory co-operation to balance these costs.
- As the UK Government works to add the measurement of trade impacts into the RIA process, the RPC will have a critical role in providing independent assurance over the robustness of the calculations and assisting in the development of the underlying methodology. In addition, the RPC could build upon its previous work to provide methodological training and guidance materials (in co-ordination with BRE and DIT) to departments and regulators. Evidence on the trade impacts of individual regulations will also be useful more generally for future trade policy.
- Broaden the scope of *ex post* review policy, by updating PIR guidance (e.g. Better Regulation Framework Guidance and other related documents such as the PIR template) to prompt departments to address inconsistency in the stock of regulation with international instruments and build on international expertise and practice. There may also be scope for joint *ex post* evaluations with key partners and greater connection with evaluation initiatives of international organisations. Box 5.7 provides example of integration of IRC considerations in *ex post* evaluation in Canada and of cross-jurisdictional reviews between Australia and New Zealand. Evidence gathered through PIRs could be leveraged to identify the priorities for the strategic IRC vision and where to target specific IRC efforts.
- In a post withdrawal context, early warnings of potential regulatory divergences and frictions with major partners are essential to inform future UK rulemaking. This calls for strengthening UK's forward planning tools that help offer information on upcoming regulations to both domestic and foreign stakeholders, including through the WTO notification process, and enabling them to provide comments (see Box 5.8). It also calls for early engagement in major partners' regulatory activities, including the EU.

---

**Box 5.4. Embedding IRC in regulatory management tools: the example of Canada and New Zealand**

In the updated version of Canada's Directive on Regulation that came into effect in September 2018, regulatory co-operation is embedded throughout the lifecycle:

- Regulators are required to assess early opportunities for alignment with other jurisdictions (domestically and internationally) to reduce unnecessary regulatory burden on Canadian businesses while maintaining or improving the health, safety, security, social and economic well-being of Canadians, and protecting the environment
- Where a Canada-specific approach is required, regulators must provide a rationale in the regulatory impact assessment statement
- Forward regulatory plans require identification of regulatory co-operation issues
- As part of stock reviews, regulators must identify new opportunities to reduce regulatory burdens on stakeholders through regulatory co-operation activities

The New Zealand Government Expectations for Good Regulatory Practice apply to all New Zealand's regulatory systems and therefore to all kinds of regulatory measures and actors.

Part A of the Expectations sets out expectations for the design of regulatory systems. This provides that "the government believes that durable outcomes of real value to New Zealanders are more likely when a regulatory system ... is consistent with relevant international standards and practices to maximise the benefits from trade and from cross border flows of people, capital and ideas (except when this would compromise important domestic objectives and values)". The term international standards in this context is used more broadly by New Zealand than in the current report, going beyond the WTO definition to cover all international instruments.

Part B sets out expectations for regulatory stewardship by government agencies. The regulatory stewardship role includes responsibilities for monitoring, review and reporting on existing regulatory systems. Regulatory agencies are expected to "periodically look at other similar regulatory systems, in New Zealand and other jurisdictions, for possible trends, threats, linkages, opportunities for alignment, economies of scale and scope, and examples of innovation and good practice".

As part of regulatory stewardship responsibilities for robust analysis and implementation support for changes to regulatory systems, regulatory agencies are expected to undertake "systematic impact and risk analysis, including assessing alternative legislative and non-legislative policy options, and how the proposed change might interact or align with existing domestic and international requirements within this or related regulatory systems".

Source: www.canada.ca/en/treasury-board-secretariat/services/federal-regulatory-management/guidelines-tools/cabinet-directive-regulation.html and https://treasury.govt.nz/sites/default/files/2015-09/good-reg-practice.pdf.

### Box 5.5. How is the need to consider international standards and other relevant regulatory frameworks conveyed in other jurisdictions

In Australia, there is a cross-sectoral requirement to consider "consistency with Australia's international obligations and relevant international accepted standards and practices" (COAG Best Practice Regulation). Wherever possible, regulatory measures or standards are required to be compatible with relevant international or internationally accepted standards or practices in order to minimise impediments to trade. National regulations or mandatory standards should also be consistent with Australia's international obligations, including the WTO Agreement on Technical Barriers to Trade and on Sanitary and Phytosanitary Measures (SPS). Regulators may refer to the Standards Code relating to the WTO TBT Agreement's Code of Good Practice for the Preparation, Adoption and Application of Standards. In addition, the Australian Government Guide to Regulation makes clear that Regulatory Impact Analysis requirements apply to the development of standards used for domestic regulatory purposes, even when developed by an independent body (such as Standards Australia) or other third parties. If a regulatory option involves establishing or amending standards in areas where international standards already apply, the proponent should document whether (and why) the proposed standards differ from the international standard. To support greater consistency of practices, the Australian government has released a publicly available Best Practice Guide to Using Standards and Risk Assessments in Policy and Regulation.

In the United States, the guidance of the Office of Management and Budget (OMB) on the use of voluntary consensus standards states that "in the interests of promoting trade and implementing the provisions of international treaty agreements, your agency should consider international standards in procurement and regulatory applications". In addition, the Executive Order 13609 on Promoting International Regulatory Cooperation states that agencies shall, "for significant regulations that the agency identifies as having significant international impacts, consider, to the extent feasible, appropriate, and consistent with law, any regulatory approaches by a foreign government that the United States has agreed to consider under a regulatory cooperation council work plan." The scope of this requirement is limited to the sectoral work plans that the United States has agreed to in Regulatory Cooperation Councils. The scope of this requirement is limited to the sectoral work plans that the United States has agreed to in Regulatory Cooperation Councils.

Source: Australian Government Guide to Regulation: https://www.pmc.gov.au/sites/default/files/publications/Australian_Government_Guide_to_Regulation.pdf; Australia COAG Best Practice Regulation Guide: www.pmc.gov.au/resource-centre/regulation/best-practice-regulation-guide-ministerial-councils-and-national-standard-setting-bodies; Australian Government Best Practice Guide to Using Standards and Risk Assessments in Policy and Regulation: https://www.industry.gov.au/sites/default/files/2019-03/best-practice-guide-to-using-standards-and-risk-assessments-in-policy-and-regulation.pdf ; US OMB Circular A 119: www.whitehouse.gov/omb/circulars_a119; US Executive Order 13609: www.gpo.gov/fdsys/pkg/fr-2012-05-04/pdf/2012-10968.pdf.

### Box 5.6. Regulatory Co-operation in Canada: a credit under one-in, one-out

Canada's Red Tape Reduction Act establishes a one-for-one rule to control the amount of administrative burden (paperwork burden) that is imposed on business through federal regulations. Whenever a new or amended regulation is brought forward by a department, it must take an equal value of administrative burden out of its regulatory stock, and must also remove a regulatory title (if a new regulation is being introduced).

In 2018, as an incentive to increase regulatory co-operation, Canada introduced amendments to the Red Tape Reduction Act to allow Canadian regulators to count reductions in administrative burden to Canadian businesses that occur in other jurisdictions, should they result from a work plan under one of Canada's three formal regulatory co-operation tables (i.e., Canada-European Union Comprehensive Economic and Trade Agreement Regulatory Cooperation Forum, Canada-United States Regulatory Cooperation Council, Federal-Provincial/Territorial Regulatory Reconciliation and Cooperation Table under the Canadian Free Trade Agreement).

### Box 5.7. Embedding IRC in *ex post* reviews in Canada and in Trans-Tasman co-operation

Canada's Cabinet Directive on Regulation requires regulators to conduct a regular review of their existing stock of regulations, including technical guidance and associated policy, to ensure that the regulations continue to be appropriate and effective and achieve their intended policy objectives. When undertaking a review, regulators must examine regulations according to a set of criteria that includes, among other things, identifying new opportunities to reduce regulatory burdens on stakeholders through regulatory co-operation activities.

In 2018, the Government of Canada announced funding over three years to conduct targeted reviews of regulatory requirements and practices that are bottlenecks to economic growth and innovation. During the first round of regulatory reviews, stakeholders highlighted the importance of regulatory co-operation and harmonization, noting that misalignment within Canada and between other international jurisdictions increases unnecessary burden on industry and acts as a barrier to trade, competitiveness, and growth.

For example, certain sectors of the agri-food industry outlined that food compositional standards are outdated, stifle innovation and are difficult to amend. Specifically, issues around the standards of production of vodka were raised. Consequently, Canada's vodka compositional standards were updated in June 2019, allowing the country's spirits industry to be more innovative, provide more choice for consumers, and enhance trade. Allowing the use of new additional agricultural products, such as honey, apple, or dairy, in vodka production has helped better align with international standards used by key trading partners, like the U.S. and European Union, which allow vodka to be produced from a wider range of materials.

The second round of targeted regulatory reviews will include a focus on international standards. By examining strategic opportunities for Canada to better incorporate international standards in regulation and accelerate its leadership in the development of international standards, this review will provide an opportunity to support regulatory streamlining and international regulatory co-operation.

The Trans-Tasman Mutual Recognition Arrangement (TTMRA) operates between Australia and New Zealand to address behind the border barriers to the movement of goods and skilled people. The TTMRA includes a specific commitment to undertake regular reviews of the operation of the arrangement and its related legislation. The TTMRA also provides that the review "will assess the effectiveness of the arrangements in fostering and enhancing trade and workforce mobility between Australia and New Zealand and should consider whether any changes to the Arrangement or related legislation are required to improve the operation or coverage of the Arrangement".

Reviews to date have been undertaken by the Australian Productivity Commission (PC). In the most recent review in 2015, the PC was asked to assess the coverage, efficiency and effectiveness of the TTMRA and recommend ways to further improve inter-jurisdictional movement of goods and skilled workers, and reduce red tape. The PC was also asked to consider other issues related to the operation of the scheme. In undertaking the study, the Commission was to consult relevant stakeholders in Australia and New Zealand, including the Cross-Jurisdictional Review Forum and to substantiate its recommendations.

Back in 2004, the PC also undertook research on the Australian and New Zealand Competition and Consumer Protection Regimes in response to a joint request by the Australian and the New Zealand governments. The objective of the study was to examine the potential to improve the trans-Tasman business environment through greater co-ordination, co-operation and integration of the Australian and New Zealand consumer protection and competition policy regimes.

Source: www.pc.gov.au/inquiries/completed/mutual-recognition-schemes#report and www.pc.gov.au/inquiries/completed/trans-tasman-consumer-protection/report/transtasman.pdf.

> **Box 5.8. Forward planning as a tool to inform domestic and foreign stakeholders in other jurisdictions**
>
> A number of OECD jurisdictions have a forward regulatory planning that can inform stakeholders, including foreign, of regulatory intents. In Canada, regulators must post their plans to develop or amend regulations over the next 24 months publicly on their websites. Each plan includes information on what regulatory co-operation efforts have been undertaken to date or that may be considered in the development of the regulatory proposal. The European Commission's work programme sets out the overall planned action for the upcoming 12 months.
>
> In Mexico, the national standardisation programme (*Programa Nacional de Normalización*, PNN) is the instrument for planning, co-ordination and information with regards to the development of technical regulations and standards. The PNN is developed by the Ministry of Economy and published in the Official Gazette once a year (a supplement can be issued mid-year) for informational purposes. On its own initiative, Mexico is the only WTO member to circulate its PNN as a WTO document to all WTO members, going beyond TBT Agreement obligations and committee recommendations. This has the benefit of giving considerable visibility to this instrument, which has the potential of serving as a baseline for early consultations, including with foreign stakeholders.
>
> Trade agreements provide additional opportunities for parties to commit to forward planning as a way to inform one another of regulatory proposals. For example, under the Canada-United States-Mexico Agreement (CUSMA), the three countries have committed to annually publishing a list of regulations that they respectively reasonably expect to propose or adopt within the next 12-month period. This list must include a description of the proposed regulation, the name of a knowledgeable contact person who could answer any questions about the proposal, an indication of sectors that could be affected, and whether there are any expected significant impacts on international trade or investment. The parties have also committed to publishing the draft legal text and regulatory impact assessment for public consultation, and have agreed that interested stakeholders from all three countries will be afforded equal opportunity to provide comments.

**Increase awareness and understanding about IRC across departments and regulators, including on the variety of existing IRC practices, and engage stakeholders to inform the development of IRC initiatives**

*Assessment*

There is uneven awareness about IRC across Departments and regulators. Some are very active in embedding international considerations in their rulemaking, whether of the EU (e.g. OfCOM) or beyond (e.g. ONR; MHRA; FCA). Overall, however, because of the absence of government policy and/or guidance on IRC, there is limited awareness about IRC and the possibility to benefit from international experience for feeding into domestic rulemaking.

The UK withdrawal from the EU has also shed light on the risk of a weakening of market surveillance and regulatory enforcement infrastructure in a context where digitalisation and other technologies are transcending borders. Going forward, the critical importance of co-operation for the proper implementation of laws and regulations needs to be more systematically emphasised and become an integral part of the enforcement policy and strategy of departments and regulators.

Various authorities co-operate actively with their foreign peers, bilaterally, regionally, plurilaterally and multilaterally. However, there is no entity within the Government that oversees or promotes IRC activities across Whitehall. The FCO has responsibility on the UK's foreign policy and oversees participation in various IOs under its authority. However, its overview is not comprehensive as the FCO does not have an overall view of individual UK authorities' participation in IOs. The FCO's role in IRC activity could be enhanced as the new Regulatory Diplomacy project develops and becomes established.

The government has organised several working groups bringing together departments and / or regulators across Whitehall on horizontal regulatory matters, e.g. BRUs; BRE Regulators Forum; Regulatory Diplomacy; Network of Economic Regulators. These working groups provide valuable opportunities for raising awareness about IRC and providing an impetus to deepen IRC efforts across the government. Nevertheless, their scale and scope remain, for the time being, limited. These networks either meet sporadically, are organised along functional organisation (independent regulators meeting separately from departments) or are seen as opportunities for information sharing from the centre. They do not yet provide a genuine opportunity for a community of practice on areas of common interest – as is the case for the Community of Federal Regulators in Canada and of the Government Regulatory Practice Initiative in New Zealand (see Box 5.9).

The withdrawal from the EU will impact upon the regulatory co-operation initiatives of departments and regulators. Beyond the participation of the UK government in the EU institutions, there is a strong intertwining of EU national regulators through various networks and bodies. They all have different governance and organisation. To prepare and deliver effective IRC following withdrawal, a mapping of various departments and regulators' situations and co-operation needs, going beyond the overview of four sectors provided in the case studies of Chapter 4, would be helpful.

Beyond the Regulatory Co-operation Council under the CETA, of which the UK is part indirectly until the end of the transition period, it does not have specific regulatory co-operation bodies (or even less formal arrangements) with any other bilateral trading partners. Going forward, these platforms can act as vectors of information and inputs, including from the stakeholder community.

*Recommendations*

- The Government should mandate the BRE to conduct a survey of existing IRC initiatives and efforts, and the approaches used across a range of departments and regulators. This survey should leverage BRE's oversight role on better regulation and its regular contacts with actors across Whitehall, the regulator community as well as the private sector. This exercise would allow highlighting positive experiences of regulators with IRC (as well as examples of where it has not been as successful), identifying Departments and/or regulatory agencies with most successful examples of IRC and giving them visibility to serve as example for other Departments and/or regulatory agencies.
- Raise awareness of IRC among departments and regulators and offer them greater incentives to make use of IRC. This could include asking departments and regulators to consolidate the information on international/foreign instruments used in a repository to help other related regulators or future administrations in their search for related references. This could also involve promoting practices such as the development of IRC strategy (following for example the model of the Office for Nuclear Regulation strategic framework for international engagement) or the systematic consideration of the risk of non-cooperation for effective policy implementation in their enforcement policy / strategy.
- Leverage existing regulators *fora* that exist in the UK government to build a community of IRC practices and other regulatory policy topics, raise awareness about IRC tools, and identify training needs when relevant. The community of practice should be an interactive platform where both

Departments and independent regulators feel safe to interact and bring the wealth of their own experience – it should not be seen as solely an information vector from the centre (Box 9).

- Create more systematic links between international units throughout Government with the FCO (perhaps through the Regulatory Diplomacy initiative) and improve information flows about active participation in IOs to give the FCO a broader view of the UK's activity in multilateral *fora*. This could enable the FCO to identify gaps and opportunities in the UK's engagement with IOs.

- Consider setting up regulatory co-operation fora with key trading partners (Box 5.10) to allow for regular exchange of information and provide opportunities for identifying the regulatory frictions and co-operation opportunities and priorities of mutual benefit (see forthcoming OECD working paper on Good regulatory practices and international regulatory cop-operation approaches in trade agreements). Such an initiative could also represent an important political commitment in support of IRC between the respective governments.

- Use regular stakeholder engagement platforms between BRE and businesses to identify regulatory frictions and specific IRC initiatives that can benefit businesses, and SMEs in particular. To do so, various business associations should be consulted for input into the design of the horizontal IRC strategy; and international SME federations in domestic consultation procedures should be targeted. To this effect, consider drawing from the lessons under Canada's interface with stakeholders in the Regulatory Co-operation Council and the Australia New Zealand Leadership Forum (Box 5.11).

---

**Box 5.9. Structuring communities of regulatory practices in Canada and New Zealand**

Canada's Community of Federal Regulators (CFR) is a partnership of Canadian regulatory organisations at the federal level that aims to facilitate professional development, collaboration and advancement of the regulatory field. The CFR focuses its events, activities and resources to meet three strategic objectives:

- Talent Management – initiatives to strengthen the regulatory profession across the system;
- Collaboration – events to connect organisations to foster collaboration and sharing of regulatory expertise;
- Experimentation – pursuing prototypes, projects and other activities to increase community understanding of innovative regulatory concepts and enabling their application.

Key activities include an annual two-day Regulatory Conference, annual one-day Law Enforcement Symposium, Regulatory Professional Development Program, Regulatory Speaker Series, Regulatory Excellence Awards, Prototyping Workshops and Communities of Practice/Working Groups on specific regulatory issues.

The community serves approximately 40 000 regulatory professionals who support Canada's regulatory lifecycle including policy analysts, program officers, compliance and enforcement officers, performance evaluators, risk assessors, legal counsel, cost-benefit analysts, amongst others. The community is governed by a Deputy Minister Champion, two Assistant Deputy Minister Co-Champions and representatives from each of the departments and agencies providing financial support to the community, responsible for setting direction and areas of focus for the community in conjunction with the CFR Office.

While much broader than IRC, the CFR awards dedicate a specific category to Excellence in Regulatory Cooperation & Collaboration. This award recognises a regulatory initiative that has demonstrated success through a collaborative or co-operative endeavour with another organisation and/or jurisdiction. Nominations must clearly highlight examples of how the candidate or team:

- demonstrated successful outcomes on a collaborative or co-operative initiative;
- produced efficiencies as a result of collaborative activities;
- improved regulatory policy or service delivery through the harmonisation, alignment and/or
- co-ordination of regulatory requirements;
- reduced duplication or redundant regulatory requirements;
- implemented an innovative method for co-operating with partners.

New Zealand Government Regulatory Practice Initiative (G-REG) is a network of central and local government regulatory agencies established to lead and contribute to regulatory practice initiatives. G-REG focuses on developing people capability, organisational capability, and building a professional community of regulators. It is a network for all regulators in the public sector, whether at central or local government.

Among other things, G-REG implements the recommendations of the New Zealand Productivity Commission, which reported in 2014 on the need "to build on the hard work and dedication of those individuals who see the practice of being a regulator as important, and who have sought to improve the capability of regulatory agencies and those that work within them".

G-REG's primary activity to date has been the development and delivery of a qualifications framework. Having a common qualification in the public sector is intended to make it easier for regulatory agencies to work together, when their people have common ways of operating and transferable skills and qualifications.

G-REG is working to unify and professionalise the regulators of New Zealand and has made the sector more aware of itself, by bringing it together through a series of workshops, in highly successful annual conferences, articles in industry journals, and intellectual credibility by establishing a Chair in Regulatory Practice at Victoria University of Wellington. Collectively this represents the development of a professional community of regulatory professionals.

The Chair in Regulatory Practice plays a crucial role in connecting the New Zealand regulatory community to the rest of world. The Chair's research programme incorporates advances in regulatory practice outside New Zealand, focusing on innovative regulators, regulatory instruments and processes. This enables international regulatory best practice and knowledge to be disseminated to G-REG and the wider regulatory community (through blogs, seminars and guest lectures), so New Zealand can learn from the rest of the world. G-REG's peer learning framework incorporates an international element by, among other things, focusing on the need to minimise the potential for unintended negative impacts of regulatory activities on regulated entities or affected supplier industries and supply chains, which are often international or regional.

G-REG is a key audience and community of knowledge for wider international regulatory co-operation initiatives in New Zealand. For example, G-REG members provided their expertise for a report on international regulatory co-operation prepared by the New Zealand Institute of Economic Research. G-REG will also be a key audience for the New Zealand IRC toolkit that is currently being developed.

### Box 5.10. Examples of international Regulatory Cooperation Fora related to trade agreements

The Canada-European Union Comprehensive Economic and Trade Agreement (CETA) establishes the Regulatory Cooperation Forum (RCF) to facilitate and promote regulatory co-operation between Canada and the European Union. The RCF considers a broad range of regulatory measures in order to improve regulatory planning, promote transparency, and enhance the efficacy of regulations by seeking to reduce duplication and misalignment. These efforts will help lower trade barriers, make it easier to do business in both markets, and improve choice for consumers. The first RCF work plan was negotiated in 2018 and contains five areas for co-operation.

Among the early RCF successes, one is the signature in November 2018 of an administrative agreement between Canada and the EC to exchange information between the EU RAPEX alert system and RADAR, Canada's consumer product incident reporting system. The exchange of information started on 5 June 2019 providing Canadian and European regulators detailed consumer product safety information. This allows for easier access to important information related to recalled products, better capacity for co-ordination of recall and/or surveillance activities, and improved collaboration between regulators of both jurisdictions in order to keep citizens safe.

The Canada-U.S. Regulatory Cooperation Council (RCC) was established in 2011 and brings together regulators from both Canadian and U.S. departments with health, safety, and environmental protection mandates to reduce unnecessary differences between their regulatory frameworks. The RCC provides a forum for stakeholders, including industry, consumers, and non-government organisations, to discuss regulatory barriers and identify opportunities for regulatory co-operation between Canada and the United State. The RCC has a two-year work planning cycle, as laid out in a Memorandum of Understanding, which includes publishing work plans, biannual reporting, and hosting a biennial forum that brings together stakeholders and senior regulators in both countries to discuss areas of misalignment and solutions to address them. The Council is co-chaired by the Secretary of the Treasury Board Secretariat and the Administrator of the U.S. Office of Information and Regulatory Affairs, and meets annually to set the high level direction and priorities.

Examples of RCC success include co-operation in relation to sunscreens. In February 2017, Canada launched a pilot project for sunscreen products manufactured in U.S. facilities that have already undergone inspection and testing by the Food and Drugs Administration, to enter into Canada without being quarantined and tested for a second time at the border. It is estimated that this regulatory co-operation initiative will save the consumer health product industry CAD 100 000 annually per sunscreen product. Due to the success of this pilot, a similar initiative was launched between Canada and the EU under the CETA-RCF in February 2019.

The depth and breadth of the trans-Tasman relationship means that there are many avenues for regulatory co-operation opportunities to be identified and discussed, both formal and informal.

The New Zealand and Australian Prime Ministers and other Ministers regularly hold formal talks, and they have frequent contact at regional and international meetings. In recognition of the close relationship between the two countries and their many shared objectives, New Zealand ministers attend some meetings of the Council of Australian Governments, Australia's highest intergovernmental forum.

Parliamentary committees, political parties, and government agencies also have strong connections. For example, a number of agencies on each side of the Tasman have arrangements in place for information sharing and dialogue, and have representation on each other's boards.

There are joint bodies such as Food Standards Australia New Zealand (FSANZ) which develops food standards for New Zealand and Australia, and Joint Accreditation System of Australia and New Zealand which is an independent third-party accreditation body established by a treaty between Australian and

New Zealand. The Regulatory Quality Team at the New Zealand Treasury and the Australian Office of Best Practice Regulation operate a protocol for commenting on Regulatory Impact Statements from the other jurisdiction that involves a trans-Tasman issue.

The Australia and New Zealand School of Government (ANZSOG) was established in 2001 by Australian and New Zealand national and state/territory-level governments, in partnership with universities and business schools, to develop strong links between our respective public sectors. ANZSOG has provided a forum for sharing experience on regulatory co-operation. See, for example, its paper Arrangements for Facilitating Trans-Tasman Government Institutional Cooperation.

### Box 5.11. Collecting views from stakeholders for more targeted IRC

Stakeholder input is a key element of the work of the Canada-U.S. Regulatory Co-operation Council (RCC). To date, there have been six written consultations and in-person events with stakeholders. The most recent event was held in December 2018 and brought together approximately 300 stakeholders and regulators to discuss advances made over the previous year and to consider priorities and ideas for the next planning cycle of RCC initiatives. According to the RCC Memorandum of Understanding, a stakeholder-regulator forum is to be held every 2 years.

In preparation for such events, Canada and the U.S. invite stakeholders to share proposals on how to address regulatory differences between the two countries. In particular, stakeholders are invited to comment on issues to be considered for future co-operation, including proposals to align existing regulatory systems, streamlining of unnecessary or duplicative procedures, and areas that will be impacted by new technologies, which are not yet regulated. In the last consultation in the lead-up to the December 2018 event, the Canadian Federation of Independent Business, which represents SMEs in Canada, provided a submission as part of this consultation. Results of the consultation process are posted publicly.

The New Zealand and Australia Leadership Forum (ANZLF) is a business-led initiative designed to further develop both the Australian and New Zealand bilateral relationship, and to provide a vehicle for direct business input into the trans-Tasman economic integration agenda. The ANZLF brings together Ministers and leaders of business, government and academia to create an independent public platform for discussing the Australia New Zealand relationship. The ANZLF has been influential in setting the trans-Tasman agenda in the past, particularly in economic matters, such as supporting the acceleration of the Single Economic Market initiative and advancing the concept of "net trans-Tasman benefit".

## Reference

OECD (2012), *Recommendation of the Council on Regulatory Policy and Governance*, http://www.oecd.org/gov/regulatory-policy/2012-recommendation.htm. [1]

## Notes

[1] They are highlighted in the OECD work on IRC. See for instance the Brochure on IRC: www.oecd.org/gov/regulatory-policy/irc.htm. Canada's Treasury Board also showcases some of the results of its IRC with the United States and others on its website: www.canada.ca/en/treasury-board-secretariat/services/regulatory-cooperation.html.

[2] www.gov.uk/government/publications/regulation-for-the-fourth-industrial-revolution.

[3] Section 30 (3) & (4) of the Small Business, Enterprise and Employment Act 2015.

# Annex A. What is international regulatory co-operation (IRC)?

The 2012 Recommendation (OECD, 2012[1]) recognises that in today's globalised context, policy makers and regulators can no longer work in isolation. They have much to learn from their peers abroad, and much to benefit from aligning approaches with them. IRC has become an essential building block to ensure the quality and relevance of regulations today. Principle 12 of the 2012 Recommendation therefore encourages countries to:

> *"In developing regulatory measures, give consideration to all relevant international standards and frameworks for co-operation in the same field and, where appropriate, their likely effects on parties outside the jurisdiction"* (OECD, 2012[1]).

Principle 12 includes the following aspects:

- Taking into account relevant international regulatory settings when formulating regulatory proposals to foster global coherence.
- Acting in accordance with international treaty obligations.
- Co-operating with other countries to promote the development and diffusion of good practices and innovations in regulatory policy and governance.
- Contributing to international fora which support greater International Regulatory Co-operation.
- Avoiding the duplication of efforts in regulatory activity in cases where recognition of existing regulations and standards would achieve the same public interest objective at lower costs.
- Opening consultation on regulatory proposals to receiving submissions from foreign interests.

Building on the Recommendation, (OECD, 2013[2]) defines IRC as any agreement or institutional arrangement, formal or informal, between countries to promote some form of coherence in the design, monitoring, enforcement or *ex post* evaluation of regulation. (OECD, 2013[2]) also highlights the different ways in which a country may approach regulatory co-operation. They range from the unilateral adoption of good regulatory practices that promote evidence-based rule-making to various co-operative approaches (bilateral, regional or multilateral) that provide for the development of common regulatory positions and instruments with other countries (Figure A A.1. ). Examples of the selected approaches and their related benefits are listed in Box A A.1.

### Figure A A.1. The variety of IRC approaches

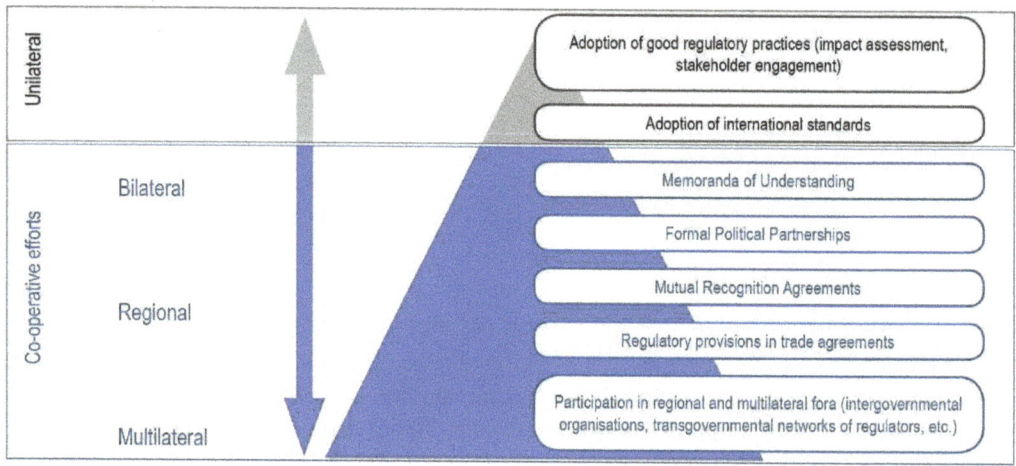

Note: unilateral approaches are pictured in grey, and collaborative approaches, ranging from bilateral to multilateral are pictured in blue.
Source: Based on (OECD, 2013[2]), International Regulatory Co-operation: Addressing Global Challenges, Paris, http://dx.doi.org/10.1787/9789264200463-en.

IRC has important implications for the activities of those who regulate and of their oversight bodies. It requires a change in the regulatory culture towards greater consideration of the international environment in the rule-making process. This involves both the more systematic review and consideration of foreign and international regulatory frameworks of relevance when regulating and the continuous assessment of how regulatory measures will impact and fit into the broader cross-border management of the issue to address. In this perspective, the regulatory management tools provide important entry points in the rule-making process to consider the international environment in the development and revision of laws and regulations. In particular, discussions in the OECD Regulatory Policy Committee[1] and further analytical work (Basedow and Kauffmann, 2016[3]) identified the following four key practices in the implementation of Principle 12.

- Practice 1: In developing regulation, systematically consider international instruments and document the rationale for departing from them in the RIA process
- Practice 2: Open consultation to foreign parties
- Practice 3: Embed consistency with international instruments as a key principle driving the review process in *ex post* evaluation
- Practice 4: Establish a co-ordination mechanism in government on IRC activities to centralise relevant information on IRC practices and activities and to build a consensus and common language.

## Box A A.1. IRC in practice: examples of approaches and related benefits

**Adoption of international standards on motorcycle regulation can help protect safety while saving millions of dollars**

On 15 September 2014, the Australian Government removed the requirement to modify rear mudguards on new motorcycles to meet unique Australian Design Rules, which imposed a requirement above the commonly accepted international rules. Abolishing this provision meant nearly 70 000 new motorcycles per annum would no longer be required to be retro-fitted with rear mudguard extensions. This is estimated to reduce regulatory burdens by AUD 14.4 million.

Source: http://minister.infrastructure.gov.au/jb/releases/2014/September/jb096_2014.aspx.

**Participation in regional organisation helped improving water quality, increasing fauna and flora and preventing floods**

The International Commission for the Protection of the Rhine (ICPR) enables co operation at the level of the Rhine river basin, including its alluvial areas and the waters in the watershed. It was formed in 1950 on a diplomatic basis between Switzerland, the Netherlands, France, Germany and Luxemburg. It was given a legal basis by the Berne Convention in 1963. The EEC joined as a member in 1976. The ICPR combines political representatives and technical experts. Over the years, it has deployed several significant benefits for the Rhine river basin:

- Improved water quality.
- Increased number of animal and plant species.
- Flood prevention.
- Ecological improvements.

Source: (Black and Kauffmann, 2013[4]), "Transboundary water management", in OECD, International Regulatory Co-operation: Case Studies, Vol. 3: Transnational Private Regulation and Water Management, Paris, http://dx.doi.org/10.1787/9789264200524-4-en.

**Participation in multilateral organisation helped enhance the effectiveness of chemical testing, with reduced costs and health and environmental gains**

The OECD Mutual Acceptance of Data system helps governments and industry save some EUR 153 million per year through reduced chemical testing and the harmonisation of chemical safety tools and policies across jurisdictions. In addition, co-operation has brought less quantifiable benefits, such as the health and the environmental gains from governments being able to evaluate and manage more chemicals than they would if working independently, the avoidance of delays in marketing new products, and the increased knowledge on new and more effective methods for assessing chemicals.

Source: (OECD, 2013[5]), Chapter 1: "Chemical safety", International Regulatory Co-operation: Case Studies, Vol. 1: Chemicals, Consumer Products, Tax and Competition, Paris, http://dx.doi.org/10.1787/9789264200487-en.

# References

Basedow, R. and C. Kauffmann (2016), "International Trade and Good Regulatory Practices: Assessing The Trade Impacts of Regulation", *OECD Regulatory Policy Working Papers*, No. 4, OECD Publishing, Paris, https://dx.doi.org/10.1787/5jlv59hdgtf5-en. [3]

Black, J. and C. Kauffmann (2013), "Transboundary water management", in *International Regulatory Co-operation: Case Studies, Vol. 3: Transnational Private Regulation and Water Management*, OECD Publishing, Paris, https://dx.doi.org/10.1787/9789264200524-4-en. [4]

OECD (2013), *International Regulatory Co-operation: Case Studies, Vol. 1: Chemicals, Consumer Products, Tax and Competition*, OECD Publishing, Paris, https://dx.doi.org/10.1787/9789264200487-en. [5]

OECD (2013), *International Regulatory Co-operation: Addressing Global Challenges*, OECD Publishing, Paris, https://dx.doi.org/10.1787/9789264200463-en. [2]

OECD (2012), *Recommendation of the Council on Regulatory Policy and Governance*, http://www.oecd.org/gov/regulatory-policy/2012-recommendation.htm. [1]

# Note

[1] 5th expert workshop on Assessing Progress in the Implementation of the 2012 Recommendation of the OECD Council on Regulatory Policy and Governance (www.oecd.org/gov/regulatory-policy/stockholm-workshop.htm) and "Key Practices for Drafting Survey Questions on the Implementation of the Recommendation: Results of Consultation With RPC Delegates", Room Document 2, 10th meeting of the Regulatory Policy Committee.

# Annex B. Sectoral coverage of mutual recognition agreements of EU

| Country | Sectors in scope | Agreement |
|---|---|---|
| Australia | Automotive products<br>Electromagnetic compatibility<br>Low Voltage Equipment<br>Machinery<br>Medical Devices<br>Pressure Equipment<br>Telecommunications terminal equipment<br>Good Manufacturing Practices for medical products | Agreement between the European Union and Australia (2012) |
| Canada | Electrical and electronic equipment, including electrical installations and appliances, and related components<br>Radio and telecommunications terminal equipment<br>Electromagnetic compatibility (EMC)<br>Toys<br>Construction products<br>Machinery, including parts, components, including safety components, interchangeable equipment, and assemblies of machines<br>Measuring instruments<br>Hot-water boilers, including related appliances<br>Equipment, machines, apparatus, devices, control components, protection systems, safety devices, controlling devices and regulating devices, and related instrumentation and prevention and detection systems for use in potentially explosive atmospheres (ATEX equipment)<br>Equipment for use outdoors as it relates to noise emission in the environment<br>Recreational craft, including their components | Comprehensive Economic and Trade Agreement (2017) |
| Israel | Good Manufacturing Practices for medicinal products | Agreement on mutual recognition of OECD principles of good laboratory practice (GLP) and compliance monitoring programmes between the European Community and the State of Israel (1999) |
| Japan | Electrical products<br>Radio and telecommunications terminal equipment<br>Good manufacturing practices for medicinal products<br>Good laboratory practices | Agreement on mutual recognition between the European Community and Japan (2001) |
| New Zealand | Good Manufacturing Practices for medicinal products<br>Electromagnetic compatibility<br>Low Voltage Equipment<br>Machinery<br>Medical Devices<br>Pressure Equipment<br>Telecommunications terminal equipment | Agreement between the European Union and New Zealand on mutual recognition in relation to conformity assessment between the European Community and New Zealand (2012) |
| Switzerland | Machinery<br>Personal Protective Equipment<br>Toys | Agreement between the European Community and the Swiss Confederation on mutual recognition in relation to conformity |

| Country | Sectors in scope | Agreement |
|---|---|---|
| | Medical Devices<br>Gas appliances and boilers (Hot water boilers)<br>Pressure vessels<br>Radio Equipment and Telecommunication Terminal Equipment<br>Equipment and protective systems intended for use in potentially explosive atmospheres<br>Electrical equipment<br>Construction plant and equipment<br>Measuring instruments and pre-packages<br>Motor Vehicles<br>Agricultural and forestry tractors<br>Good Laboratory Practice – GLP<br>Medicinal products, Good Manufacturing Practice (GMP), inspection batch and certification<br>Construction products<br>Lifts<br>Biocidal products<br>Cableways<br>Explosives for civil use | assessment (2012) |
| United States | Electromagnetic compatibility<br>Telecoms<br>Good Manufacturing Practices for medicinal products<br>Marine Equipment | Agreement on mutual recognition between the European Community and the United States of America (1999)<br>Agreement between the European Community and the United States of America on the Mutual Recognition of Certificates of Conformity for Marine Equipment (2004) |

Source: Information provided by UK Office of Product Safety and Standards. See also: https://ec.europa.eu/growth/single-market/goods/international-aspects/mutual-recognition-agreements_en.

Lightning Source UK Ltd.
Milton Keynes UK
UKHW050633190520
363475UK00001B/2